Cra(Theft Rings

The Story of a Cop at the Port of Halifax

Jim,
Billy Taylor

by Billy Taylor with Andrew Safer

Jim,
Your warriorship is very much appreciated. Thanks for your assistance.
Andrew Safer

Frontlist
PUBLISHING

CRACKING THE THEFT RINGS
THE STORY OF A COP AT THE PORT OF HALIFAX

Published by Frontlist Publishing

Typeset, printed, and bound in Canada.

Cover photographs: Robert Norwood Collection, Courtesy of Nova Scotia Archives and Records Management

Cover design: Lisa Neily

ISBN 978-0-7795-0254-7

I DEDICATE THIS BOOK TO MY WIFE

Carol Anne (Dauphinee) Taylor
Born in Bedford, Nova Scotia on March 25th, 1936
Died in Sackville, Nova Scotia on May 12th, 1990
You are my every thought,
Every day, every hour, every minute.

ACKNOWLEDGMENTS

I would like to thank the people who helped make this book possible.

Suzanne Townsend, editor, read my original manuscript and edited a chapter to send to The Writers' Union of Canada. They said there was good material for a book, but it needed to be rewritten. Suzanne referred me to Andrew Safer, my co-writer, who I would like to thank for his time, patience, and professionalism.

Shawn O'Hara of Ferrier Dumke Kimball Thomas, Bridgewater, is my lawyer who reviewed the manuscript more than once (!) and gave us very good legal advice. Alan Parish, Q.C. of Burchell Hayman Parish, Halifax also provided expert legal advice.

James Gimian, Suzanne Townsend, Bill Turpin, Ken Friedman, Catherine Safer, Silver Donald Cameron, Jane Buss, Steph Jordan, Don Hogan, and Susie Barbour reviewed the manuscript (at various stages) and provided very helpful suggestions and advice. Alex Smith provided valuable feedback on the cover.

My good friends, Eric Mott, Kempton Hayes, Roger Miller, Bruce Brine, and Ron, my sponsor, never gave up on me OR the book. I'd like to thank them for their encouragement.

Ron Backman reviewed sections of the book at various times.

Freda Atkinson was a strong believer in this book. Even though she has passed away, I'd like to thank her for her belief in me and the project.

My son, Steven, has been very helpful coordinating the transfer of photos and drafts with Andrew Safer. My daughter-in-law, Lysia Taylor, designed an early book cover and photographed some of my prized possessions.

Lisa Neily, graphic designer, worked with us patiently, over time, in designing the cover. Jennifer Prozesky scanned the photos, Nancy Roberts guided us through the publishing process, and Frontlist Publising brought this book into the world!

Nova Scotia Archives and Records Management provided access to historic photographs of the Port of Halifax.

CONTENTS

While all the events in *Cracking the Theft Rings* are true, some of the names have been changed to protect the privacy of individuals.

This book, including much of the dialogue, has been written from my memory and records of events in my life. Every effort has been made to ensure accuracy.

Although some of the longshoremen, stevedores, checkers, cops, and other port workers written about here were involved in waterfront theft, many were not. There is no intention, express or implied, to malign these professions.

Billy—father, husband, brother, wrestler, referee, cop, and private investigator. What a hell of a mixture to write about! His life is like no other. He overcame alcohol addiction, the loss of both his wife, and later, a companion, and the deaths of his grandson and one son. He even planned to kidnap his nephew's son who went missing at the age of three.

He grew up in a dirt-floor basement apartment and worked his whole life providing for those he loved. He was successful in his career, advancing to the rank of sergeant and passing some of the toughest training courses in the police department—with his Grade Five education!

But Billy was no saint. It was frustrating working with him because, like most alcoholics, he was inconsistent and unpredictable. To mask the alcohol smell on his breath, he used to eat garlic, but not just a clove at a time. He chewed on the whole bulb!

I went to work for the Halifax Port Police in 1975. At that time there were twenty-seven men on the force. I figure only a quarter of them wanted to do police work. The rest were there for their paycheques. That worked out well for the administration because they just wanted us to write parking tickets, report when lights burned out, and take care of other minor duties. Any more than that and we might interfere with the shipping.

In the late 1970s, we noticed that the drug trade coming in through the Port of Halifax started to change—from marijuana and hashish, to mainly hashish and cocaine. Customs was checking only three percent of the containers, and we didn't have any scanners or dogs. We knew from informants that a lot was getting through, but management didn't have the will to address the issue.

The theft of goods has always been a way of life on the waterfront. There were theft rings involving some of the stevedores, checkers, watchmen, cargo repairmen, truckers, freight handlers, ships' crews and chandlers, fish plant, cold storage plant and grain elevator workers, Ports Canada staff, and cops. Some of the white-collar port workers were in on it too. Before containerization, you'd see one group, such as stevedores, protecting boxes of liquor, shoes, fire-arms, and the like from other groups of workers. "It's not *theirs* to steal," they'd say. "It's *ours* to steal!" They became more efficient after containerization, when they could steal the whole container, and with the help of two-way radios, they were more organized. Sometimes, groups would co-operate. Most of the cops who were involved would simply look the other way in exchange for a payoff.

Billy made one thing clear to everyone on the waterfront. "If I ever catch one of you taking things," he'd say, "I'll have you charged, and fired!' He himself never took as much as a cup of coffee or a donut. Billy earned everything he ever got.

There was no shortage of serious police work at the Port—just a shortage of cops and administrators who gave a damn. Billy and a few of us didn't mind sticking our noses into whatever was going on, and getting in hot water for it. If they wanted to reprimand us or fire us, they'd call Ottawa, and Ottawa would call our boss—but that never stopped us.

Well done, Billy. You've completed your dream—this book.

I know God put you in my path for a reason, and I'm glad He did.

Eric Mott
Sackville, Nova Scotia

INTRODUCTION

Billy Taylor seems like a character out of a dramatic movie, but he's flesh and blood. As RCMP Sergeant Joe Rogers of Fredericton once said: "Billy, you're the kind of man that poets and songwriters write about..."

When we met twelve years ago, he had been in recovery through Alcoholics Anonymous for a couple of years. Despite the fact that he couldn't read or write until the age of twenty-five, he had written a book and was looking for a writer to work with him on the manuscript.

Billy is salt of the earth. At seventy-six, he's short, built like a tank, and reeks of pipe tobacco. He's street smart and looks you straight in the eye. The wrinkles in his weathered face tell you he's had a hell of a life, and he has a boatload of stories to tell.

He was born on August 7, 1932 on Morris Street in Halifax. As a professional wrestler and wrestling referee on television, Billy rubbed shoulders with some of the world's greatest wrestlers, as well as grapplers who were involved with organized crime. In these pages he explains what it means to be a blade runner and a shooter—well-guarded secrets of the wrestling business.

During the thirty-one years he worked as a cop at the Port of Halifax, cargo theft was rampant. In the days before containerization, when goods were piled to the rafters in the storage sheds, it was easy for a few boxes to go missing. Writing off merchandise as damaged goods and then distributing the items to port workers was a popular sport. Billy was one cop who couldn't be corrupted, and he went after these crooks—sometimes on his own. The challenge of penetrating the theft rings at the Port is what got him out of bed in the morning.

His efforts set a precedent for prosecuting the theft of goods in transit in Nova Scotia. Eventually he got past the obvious targets—the stevedores, checkers, and other port workers—and began to nail cops and managers. That was the beginning of the end. It's a modern-day David and Goliath story, with a predictable ending.

For Billy, with each victory came tragedy or defeat—both at work and in his personal life. His best friend was alcohol, which accompanied him into the locker room after wrestling matches as a teen, and into the depths of despair much later, after his wife died. The grit and determination that made him a formidable wrestler and cop pulled him through.

Cracking the Theft Rings is a vivid, close-up view of the seedy side of port life, the creativity of crooks, and a striking chronicle of one man's struggle to overcome tremendous obstacles.

Andrew Safer
Dartmouth, Nova Scotia

1. "BRIGHT EYES" FREDDIE

I left the police station at around seven-thirty and headed over to Pier 20 for a routine check on the night lights and to secure the building. It was a dark winter night and the port city of Halifax was unusually cold—even for January.

A light snow had sprinkled the parking lot. Starting at Pier 20, I made my way to the electrical department stores and the freight-handlers hiring hall. When I reached Pier 22 I could make out a double row of boxcars on the track side (nearest the shed) and about fifteen cars in the parking lot. One of the boxcars was parked even with the shed. Portable ramps had been placed in between the shed and the boxcar. The forklift drivers used these ramps to move the goods into the cars. Curious whether the boxcars were loaded or empty, I cut across the parking lot towards Pier 23 for a better look.

Just then I spotted the soft glow of a light underneath the boxcar. Not knowing what the hell that could be, I figured maybe the light was coming from inside Shed 22 through a broken track-side door. I was about to call this in on the radio when I heard something move under the boxcar.

'I bet a CNR (Canadian National Railroad) brakeman is getting ready to make a shunt,' I thought, as I walked around the end car and alongside the shed. The third shed door was raised up about two feet, like it was stuck open. I walked closer so I could make out the number on the door, to report it to maintenance. A dozen or so cardboard boxes were scattered on the ground just outside the opening.

I was craning my neck, trying to read the painted black numbers on the shed door. Just then, someone appeared about fifteen feet away.

It was Freddie.

We knew him as Bright Eyes because his eyes were slanted, squinty, and wild. In the feeble light I peered at Freddie's piercing eyes. He was startled—and angry. Freddie was a foot taller and fifty pounds heavier than me. He would take advantage of his size any way he could.

Caught off guard, I stood there for a moment, noticing his coveralls, web belt, and khaki winter jacket.

It was a break and enter in progress, and Freddie wasn't the type to run.

His right hand crossed his torso and grabbed his cotton hook[1]. Raising it high in the air above his right shoulder, he barked in a menacing tone: "TAYLOR, YOU LITTLE PRICK."

A car horn shrieked. Must be coming from the parking lot directly behind me. Probably Jake, Freddie's partner. Jake could be closing in on me from behind right now, I thought, but I don't dare take my eyes off Freddie.

I shuffled my feet to get a better look at him, and to buy some time.

Wild eyed, clenching his jaws and gritting his teeth, Freddie took a few steps toward me holding the hooked knife steady overhead. I reached down and pulled out my revolver. Grasping it with both hands, I pointed it at the bastard.

He was just six feet away.

As I held the gun on him, I stared into Freddie's eyes to see if he was about to make a move. You can always tell by the eyes.

"DROP THE HOOK," I yelled in my ugliest voice.

Nothing.

"I SAID, DROP THE HOOK!" I yelled, louder.

Freddie was breathing hard. He was blowing on me, we were so close. I could smell booze on him.

My sights were pointed at his kill zone, smack in the centre of his chest. If he were any farther away I could shoot one of his legs, but at this distance, I'd have to take him out. At this close range, with a leg wound Freddie could still lunge forward and hook me.

"DROP THE HOOK, YOU BASTARD, OR I'LL BLOW YOU ALL OVER THE SIDE OF THE SHED!"

Sensing I was bluffing, he inched closer. With my left thumb, I cocked the hammer. Freddie froze when he heard the click, and I started to come unglued.

My mind was racing. The cops had just put me through a hell of a lot of psychological testing, and I wasn't supposed to be carrying a gun. I recalled Sections 25 and 26 of the Criminal Code which guard against the excessive use of force. I knew with the mushroomed lead bullet tips—"Plus P" ammo—there

---

1 A six-inch steel hook encased in a wooden handle that longshoremen used to grab and move large cartons, raw rubber, and other bulk items.

would be tremendous explosive power on contact. If a bullet entered Freddie's chest, it would tear a hole a foot in diameter, exit his back, and blow him all over the shed siding.

Still pointing my gun at Freddie I knew that if I pulled the trigger, I'd be a goner because I'd have to take a sobriety test. I'd had a few doubles of rye at home and polished off half a dozen beers at the tavern before coming on shift. I'd definitely fail the test.

Just when I had him, I was losing my nerve.

I wanted to throw my gun down and walk away. Screw it! It's not worth it, after all the shit I've been through over guns. I was just about to give up when Freddie brought his arm down and tossed the hook to the ground. Just then I could feel something inside me give way. My pants were starting to get wet in front. Soon, it was trickling down my leg. The big bad cop was pissing himself! Luckily, it was too dark for Freddie to see.

"Now, turn around and face the shed," I barked in as tough a voice as I could manage under the circumstances. "You're under arrest, Freddie, for B&E."

When he crossed his hands behind his back, I knew it was over.

Tucking my revolver back into its holster, I slapped on the cuffs and walked Freddie over to my police cruiser.

That was the winter of 1974, my sixteenth year as a port cop.

2. BEGINNINGS

The phone rang and I walked over to pick it up--*slowly*, like the eighteen-year-old punk I was—as if to say, 'I couldn't care less.'

My "Hullo?" was automatic and expressionless, to let the caller know that I didn't give a good goddamn who they were.

"This is Len Hughes," boomed back at me. His voice was raspy and self-assured.

Len Hughes! WOW!

I was overwhelmed...speechless, at first.

Secretly, I had been hoping Len would call for almost a year. A top wrestler in his day, Len was now a booker who promoted wrestling matches throughout the Maritimes. A year earlier he was the big name wrestler on a card with Bill Rhyno. My buddy, Al Zinck, and I were on that same card. It was at a match in New Germany, back in 1951.

This was one of my first wrestling
matches, in 1951.
They threw in a dance after the match!
Bridgewater Bulletin.

Afterwards, we all rode back to Halifax in Len's car.

I remember Len turning around to say, "That was a helluva show you guys put on tonight. I expected to see a wrestling match, not a goddamn war!"

Al and I had started wrestling at exhibitions and fairs when we were sixteen. By this time, we were putting on a pretty good show—roughhouse style, but we decided the outcome of the match in advance. Al was the hero; I was the villain. The fans ate it up.

A wrestling match on McNab's Island in 1948. The tents in the background were the dressing rooms and first-aid quarters. Left to right: Al Zinck, Ronnie Mayfield, and Curly Elguire, Referee (standing).
I took on the winner of this match.
Photographer unknown.

We had been wrestling at exhibitions and fairs every week between May and October for two years, and I was ready to move on to pro wrestling. But that wasn't a step I could take on my own. I needed a Len Hughes to open the door.

"Oh, hello Len!" I replied coolly, wondering for the life of me what this was about.

He cleared his throat and got right to the point. "How would you like to wrestle at the Arena this coming week?"

'YAHOOO!' a voice inside wanted to shout, but I squelched it. This was like asking a hockey player if he wanted to play in the NHL! "Definitely," I said.

"I'm ready any time." I started to pace in the narrow hallway in my parents' bungalow.

"Is Al still around?" Len asked.

"Oh, yeah," I said. "He is."

"OK. I'll book you and Al in the opening bout on Friday night." Len had an unmistakable air of authority.

"Thanks, Len. That's great!"

"If this works out, there will be more work for you and Al." Len was experimenting with us to see if he could use some of the local guys, instead of always bringing in wrestlers from Toronto, Montreal, and the US eastern seaboard.

"I'm sure you'll be pleased," I assured him.

When Len hung up I felt like doing cartwheels but instead I went into the kitchen to break the news to my mom. "I'm going to wrestle at the Shirley Street Arena with the big name wrestlers," I told her with pride, if not cockiness.

"Well, that's nice," Mom said evenly. "Now, don't get hurt."

I headed out the front door and up Dutch Village Road for a long walk.

It felt like Christmas! OK, so now I've got my foot in the door. I just have to prove myself. Moneywise, the sky's the limit. I could see making $20,000 a year some day out of this. And everyone will respect me. People will know who Billy Taylor is. They'll know not to mess with me. I'll have all kinds of money. I'll meet a beautiful girl—and get even with Florence.

Florence was the fourteen-year-old Shirley Temple I fell for in Grade Five. Her dynamite looks and the way she dressed hooked me. She was rich and she was my first true love. I couldn't take my eyes off her whenever she was around. On Florence's birthday, I delivered a gift to her sprawling home "on the other side of the tracks" the day before her birthday party, hoping she would invite me in. Instead, she showed up at my door several hours later to return the gift. She told me I couldn't come to the party because she didn't want to be seen with anyone dressed as shabbily as me. Besides, I was poor! I didn't belong.

After this early rejection, I swore off girls for years.

As I turned the corner to cross the railroad tracks I was imagining a spankin' new dark blue Chrysler. A lot of the wrestlers drove Chryslers, and I was going to have me one. I was going to wear dress clothes, too—not the hand-me-downs I had worn all my life. And I'd be able to help my parents. I knew Billy Taylor would never be anyone's hero since I'd always be the villain, and I was OK with that. It wasn't fame I was after. It was money —and respect.

My grandmother had come within a hair's breadth of going from rags to riches, so I figured with a little luck, I might just pull it off and change my family's fortunes.

When I was eight my mom told me how difficult it had been for her mother, Mary, to provide for her three children. The widow's only source of income, housecleaning, brought in seventy-five cents to a dollar a day. Every Friday she would have to walk all over Halifax to collect her wages, and some customers would put her off until the next week. Her debts piled up, and she was later charged under the Indigent Debtors Act.

My grandmother, Mary Earl, with my mother, Alice, 1914.

Grandma appeared before the judge to plead her case, and, unimpressed, the judge sentenced her to two weeks in debtor's prison, which was then housed at the Courthouse on Spring Garden Road near downtown Halifax. But Grandma had connections. The jailer had been a housecleaning customer of hers, so she worked a deal to serve her time cooking meals for the inmates. The only time she spent in the jail cell was when she slept! Even so, her two-week sentence passed slowly and painfully since she was separated from her children.

Years later, a distant cousin who lived in London, England died and left an estate worth millions. Grandma was the only survivor of the "Earl" family, so she figured the inheritance would be hers. While trying to prove her ancestry, she discovered that the church where she had been baptized had burned to the ground. All of the records had been destroyed, and there was no central registry at that time. She retained the law firm of Longley & Longley who sent a lawyer to London to argue her case. Producing a family Bible with Grandma's name written inside would have been sufficient proof of her bloodline, but no such Bible existed. The fortune escaped Grandma's grasp.

In 1938 Grandma slipped and fell in her bathtub, broke her jaw, and died of shock the following day. She was given a pauper's burial in Camp Hill Cemetery.

And now Billy Taylor had a chance to make up for her bad luck. I would make good!

When I walked into work at eight o'clock the next morning, I could hardly bear another day of drudgery. Cooped up behind a meat counter—I just couldn't take this much longer. At fifty-five cents an hour, sixty-five hours a week brought in a measly thirty-five dollars and seventy-five cents. On top of that, I had to work from eight to nine in the morning getting the display cases set up, and twenty minutes at the end of each day washing them out—without pay.

That Friday, I couldn't keep my mind on my work. I may as well have been counting down the hours and minutes to my first trip to Disneyland.

I showed up at the Arena dressing room an hour early and changed into my wrestling gear. I was sitting on the bench when Al Korman from Toronto and Bull Curry from Hartford, Connecticut walked in.

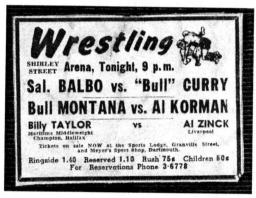

For wrestling Al Zinck at the Shirley Street Arena in 1951, I was paid $25. Police and firemen working this event were paid $3.
The Halifax Mail and *The Halifax Herald*.

Al was a carbon copy of Edward G. Robinson but he was more heavyset, probably 230 pounds and only 5' 8". Quiet and soft-spoken, he was a villain who looked the part—the type no one would want to cross. He was the villain I wanted to imitate.

Bull made me nervous because I'd seen him perform in the ring. A street fighter, he was a puncher, not a wrestler. He could hold his fist six inches from your jaw, snap it so you wouldn't even see his fist move, and knock you out. Very dark skinned, he had as much hair on his eyebrows as I had on my whole head.

When they walked in, Bull said, "You don't seem to be old enough to be a wrestler. You look more like a junior delinquency." (Bull's English wasn't very good, but I wasn't about to correct him!)

I had only seen these guys from the bleachers before. I introduced myself and the next minute I was sitting with them, talking as if we had been friends for years.

Just before the match, Len came in to have a few words with me.

In his mid-forties, Len was the businessman behind the sport. He stood 6' 2" and weighed about 250 pounds. His cauliflower ears showed that he had paid his dues in the ring. Well educated, he wore a Clark Gable moustache that gave him an air of importance. Len's extremely good looks, personality, and unusually stylish dress impressed me right off the bat.

Len Hughes was a wrestler before he became a promoter. He
gave me this photo in 1952.
Photographer unknown.

When Len first came to Halifax to wrestle, he was the "Masked Marvel". No one could defeat him to unmask him. Finally, Red Mephisto put a bad beating on Len in a match at the Halifax Wanderer's Grounds and tore his mask off. World War Two had just broken out and Len returned to his home in Mount Cisco, New York where he promptly joined the US Navy. After the war he came back to Halifax to be a wrestler and booker.

"Now Billy," Len said in a no-nonsense tone, "this match here, you and Al go Broadway." I had heard this term before. It meant to stretch things out or wrestle up to the time limit (to a draw). I nodded and he went to the other dressing room to tell Al.

Al was in the dressing room with the so-called heroes ("baby faces"). They put the heroes and villains in two different dressing rooms to make it look like they couldn't plan the match. Al and I were up first. I was confident, but as soon as I heard the announcer's voice over the loudspeaker, I felt nauseous.

"Billy Taylor, weight 175 pounds, from Armdale, and Al Zinck, 173 pounds, from Liverpool. This is the opening bout of the evening: a one-fall, twenty-minute time limit. Introducing from Armdale, at 175 pounds, the Maritime middle-weight wrestling champion, Billy Taylor, and his opponent, from Liverpool, Nova Scotia, at 173 pounds, the challenger, Al Zinck."

When we met in the centre of the ring, I glanced around and saw that the Arena was full. That meant there were about 4,000 fans in the bleachers. The referee brought us into a huddle and did his best to put us at ease. "Don't get nervous now, fellas," he said. "Take your time. I know you're going to do a good job here tonight. Start off slow. Don't burn yourselves out in the first five min-utes because you have to go to the limit. Now, go back to your corners."

At the bell, we started right in, using all the moves we knew. Billy the villain put Al in the ropes right from the start. I waited until the full count of four to break and then, holding his head by the hair, I gave him a belt with my fist to show I didn't wrestle clean. We took hard thumps on the mat and threw each other into the ring buckles to the sound of the fans' cheers and boos. After a few false finishes, we ended in a draw. We kept the match going the full twenty minutes, as Len had said. The fans got their money's worth.

Back in the dressing room after my shower, Len walked in.

"You did a good job, Billy," he said. "Both you guys had a good match."

"You did great," Bull added. "You guys get a little more weight on, and you'll be wrestling anybody."

Len paid once a week, but since it was the end of the week, he handed me twenty-five dollars in cash on the spot.

Holy crap! I had just made twenty-five dollars for twenty minutes' work! That's seventy-five dollars an hour!

It was like winning the lotto.

I stuffed the bills in my left pants pocket, and, carrying my wrestling bag, walked home.

My mother, father, and younger brother Dave were sitting in the living room when I walked in.

"How'd it go?" Dave asked.

"It went good; we wrestled to a draw."

I wasn't about to tell them the match was fixed. I rationalized that it was only half-fixed because of the way Al and I wrestled. With the money I was making, I was happy to play dumb.

Before I hit the big time, my life had been far from glamorous. I was poor, dressed shabbily, and was a loner. My father was hardly ever home. (A chauffeur for Senator William H. Dennis, he was usually at the Senator's twenty-three room mansion in Princeport, Nova Scotia, or in Ottawa). I couldn't read or write and wound up dropping out of school in Grade Six. I didn't give a good goddamn about anything—except fighting.

The fighting in my life started when I was born. I was the result of an unplanned pregnancy, which forced my parents to marry for the wrong reasons. Back in 1932, a Protestant marrying a Catholic didn't make matters any easier.

My mother, Alice Mary LeDrew (Taylor), 1931.
My father, William Stanley Taylor (front), 1942.
Photographers unknown.

Dad's in-laws (from his first marriage) strongly disapproved of the marriage. In fact, they would not allow their grandchildren to be raised by a Protestant stepmother. In the end, they compromised by letting my half-brother Wilfred and older half-sister Eleanor, who were in their early teens, stay at our home, and they took my younger half-sister Dorothy, who was nine, to be raised under their roof.

When Dad's first wife, Elizabeth, died at twenty-nine, he was unable to both work and look after their three children, so he turned to his mother and father-in-law for help. Afterwards, he always felt indebted to them. I thought of him as a "people pleaser" for letting someone else dictate where one of his children would live, and how she was to be raised.

It wasn't until years later that I realized that in the Hungry Thirties, when there was no welfare or Employment Insurance like there is today, Dad might have actually made the right decision. That way, at least he knew she would be clothed, fed, and looked after.

I remember when Dad, Mom, and I used to go to visit Dorothy at the in-laws'. They wouldn't let Mom in the house! She had to wait in the car. My little mind couldn't fathom why my mother was being kept from Dorothy, and I couldn't bear to see the tears Dorothy shed when we left.

Some of my parents' fights were about Dorothy, some were about religion, and some were about how hard it was just getting by.

My mother resented her stepchildren, my father resented my mom for being Protestant, and, when I was a young boy, I figured he resented me because I was the reason they got married. As a baby, my first memory of home is of my parents shouting. My response was to build elaborate roads in the dirt floor of our basement apartment on Morris Street. As a toddler, one of my earliest memories was of Mom throwing Dad's clothing into the coal furnace and burning every stitch he owned except what he was wearing. I wondered why she would do such a thing. I got used to squeezing my three-year-old hands over my ears to block out the screaming. As I grew older, I never invited anyone to my home because I didn't want them to see what was going on in my family. That's one reason I didn't have any friends.

I was always about six inches shorter than the other boys my age, who would say "You forgot to grow," and "You must have gotten wet and shrunk." Maybe they were just kidding, but their jeers hurt. I soon found a way to gain their respect: whenever we'd wrestle, I'd win.

I started my wrestling career at the age of twelve, on front lawns around town. Already lifting weights, I was unusually strong for my age and didn't mind showing it. I came by wrestling honestly because my grandfather used to support his womanizing and boozing by challenging men to fights in the towns of Westville, Stellarton, Pictou, and Antigonish. He always did well because he was an exceptionally good boxer and wrestler.

Granddad left home after his fifth child was born (my dad was the second). My dad doesn't remember seeing him before he was sixteen. That was in 1910. He came across his father, 6' 4" and 280 pounds, heaving a pick in a New Glasgow coal mine. Dad moved in with Granddad. Not long after, Dad began to go with him on his boxing and wrestling tours, where he looked after the betting. In those days, Granddad's impromptu matches were held either in an open field or in a barn. It was winner takes all, and Dad would place the bets whenever someone was willing to take on my grandfather—who never lost a match.

These were the days of Prohibition, when it was illegal to purchase liquor except under special circumstances, such as for sacramental wine. Granddad smelled the opportunity and, using the windfall from a particularly profitable fight, he set himself up in a new business.

My father told me Granddad was one of Nova Scotia's most notorious bootleggers and rumrunners. His career spanned over thirty years, from the late 1800s to the 1930s. Details of his operation are sketchy but he did most of his business from inlets in Guysborough and Pictou where US ships landed the precious cargo, in the days before the Nova Scotia Liquor Commission. Some of the more entrepreneurial individuals who had been licensed to brew ale or spirits for their own use began to sell liquor either to a bar, or to a speakeasy in the back of a hotel. Granddad sold direct to coal miners. In order to ensure the cooperation of the cops and the politicians, he opened a whorehouse on the side. Even though this bought him protection for awhile, he ended up serving federal time in Dorchester Penitentiary for bootlegging.

Inheriting Granddad's genes only explains part of my fighting streak. The fights in my household had more to do with poverty than bloodlines. I was born right smack in the Depression years and we were always poor. My father kept us clothed and fed as best he could—on the salary of a gardener, handyman, and chauffeur—but seven kids were a lot of mouths to feed. When there was no work, he'd leave the house at five a.m. and head for the South End, the wealthier part of the city, to steal milk bottles off front steps so we could be fed. In the wintertime, he used to steal wood and coal to heat our home. I often went along for the ride and saw that when he bought a bag of coal, he'd load an extra two while he was at it, hiding them in the back of the truck.

Each week a different bill collector would knock on our door. More often than not either our lights or our phone was cut off, and we only had basic food staples. There was never money for clothing so I'd often have to wear hand-me-downs, which wouldn't have been so bad if they weren't my sisters'! I'd have to wear girls' jackets and shoes to school when I was seven and eight years old. No wonder I got teased! That's why I didn't want to go to school, and why I spent over half my time playing hooky. Between being picked on at school and the fighting at home, schoolwork was the least of my worries. In fact, I didn't learn how to read and write until I was twenty-five.

My frustration at school gave me another reason to fight. A star student at oral exams, I came in first when asked to name the major oceans of the world, all of the counties in Nova Scotia, or the Province's capital. But whenever the teacher would give us a written test, I failed. In fact, I wouldn't write anything down on paper and when asked to explain myself, I had no excuse. I didn't say a word, which upset my teachers even more. Finally, in Grade Three at Sir John Thompson School, I loudly refused to take a written test. My impatient teacher called me "rebellious" and "stupid" in front of the class. She made me come up to the front of the room, strapped me, and told me to stay after school. She sure taught me!

That Friday, we did finger painting in Art class—one of my favourite subjects. I painted a sailboat on blue waves rimmed with white caps, with the sun setting in the background. The kids sitting near me were admiring my painting when the teacher came over to see our work. After studying mine for a while, she picked it up and said, "What is this supposed to be?" It was obvious, but I explained it to her. She took it to her desk where she kept looking at it. Finally, she tore it into pieces and threw it in the waste can, without saying another word.

I figured maybe she was getting back at me because I hadn't shown up at the after-school concert the week before. I would have had to wear my hand-me-down clothes and my sister's shoes and I couldn't bear it. I had a good singing voice so I must have been missed. I hadn't explained my absence, so I figured she was teaching me a lesson.

I never did get on track with schoolwork. Partway through Grade Six, when I was thirteen, my teachers met with my parents and suggested that I'd probably be better off doing something else. Earl Withrow, the Principal at Quinpool Road School, told them, "Billy's a very smart boy—but not in school."

As I said, fighting was in my genes. My dad had lived his life a very angry man—at God and the churches, and he blamed God for most of his problems. He would stomp out into the backyard, look up at the sky, and shake his fist at God. He would defy God to come down and face him, to settle the score over the breakup of his family, once and for all.

That image always haunted me. I never knew if God was on my side, or if He was sitting up there mocking me.

One Sunday in the middle of summer, a group of children joined our congregation because a fire had closed their church. They were from the poor sections of the city and were not allowed inside because the girls didn't have hats and the boys didn't have ties. I thought that was ridiculous! I watched as a man tied a handkerchief around a little girl's head and said, "There, now you have a hat; go on inside." I knew how embarrassed she must have felt. When I left church that day, I stayed away for two years.

At sixteen I did an about-face. I decided to become a minister and went back to church to take Bible studies. I figured as a minister I could change the rules so that anyone could pray to God. I would pray to God to become tall and rich. Soon, I began to ask myself: How is it that I am doing His work, and He is not answering my prayers? I began to see God in a different light: how could He let there be wars, genocide, and starving children? I concluded that He was not a loving God of mercy at all; He was a God of revenge and punishment. I figured that since God hadn't delivered, He must hate me and, in return, I hated Him. This is a secret I kept most of my life.

Since God wasn't on my side, I had to do my damnedest to stick up for myself. That's when I got serious about wrestling.

My strength, endurance, and stamina had become obvious in my early teens when I excelled in baseball, football, running, weightlifting, and boxing. I held wrestling titles in the Nova Scotia, Maritime, and Canadian Amateur Wrestling Championships in the lightweight and middleweight divisions. Wrestling was my life.

Both exercise and diet were key. I ate mainly vegetables, fruits, whole grain cereals and breads, meat, fish, and healthy desserts. In addition to high roughage foods, I used to eat raisins and molasses for iron, and bananas and green peppers for potassium. These high-energy foods gave me staying power.

Every day, I would soak my hands and face with a solution of water and coarse salt, and rub it over my upper body. This was Granddad's skin-toughening technique that my father had passed on to me. With his leathery skin, Granddad never bled in a bare-fisted boxing match. For me, it prevented mat burns. Whenever I was about to get caught in a wrestling hold I would spin out of it on my back, knee or elbow, without getting a mat burn. This gave me the edge in a match because I could escape and use counter holds, which is half the battle in wrestling.

My first break came when I was invited to watch a pro match at the Shirley Street Arena in Halifax. I felt at home among the yelling, the stink of bodies, the triumph, and the loss.

It wasn't long before my buddy Al Zinck and I were "barnstorming" all over Atlantic Canada— holding wrestling matches in barns or open fields in true Taylor style.

Myself (left) and Al Zinck (right) on McNab's Island, 1948
Photographer unknown.

Myself and Al in Sackville, 1992.
Photographer unknown.

We went to county fairs and exhibitions and promoted ourselves for matches with local wrestlers. Because our only expenses were gas for the car and lunches, we only charged adults twenty-five cents, and children ten cents. Our ads read: "Take On All Comers", and we paid five dollars to anyone who could last five minutes in a match with either of us.

The lumberjacks, fishermen, and other "tough guys" who rose to the bait lacked speed, timing, wind, endurance, and staying power. We never lost. The tactic I used was to wind my opponent, grab hold of him, and then yell a meaningless string of words at him: "FIRM BRANCH. KEY SIDE. WEE SIDE." The poor guy would look at me blankly, and lose his concentration. It worked every time. Sometimes I'd chew a large clove of garlic and then get close to him and breathe heavily in his face. That too wrecked his concentration. Sometimes Al and I would come home with as much as ten or twelve dollars in our pockets.

Some sixty years later, while working on this book, I was curious what my boyhood buddy and doctor, Kempton Hayes, would say about the kind of kid I was back then so I paid him a visit. Kemp came from a well-to-do family but since we lived in the same neighbourhood, we used to chum around.

Left to right: Myself, Bill Langley, Kempton Hayes, Mannie Bowdridge.
Clinton Avenue, Armdale, Halifax, 1948.
Photographer unknown.

Sitting on the couch in the family room of his nicely furnished home in the West End of Halifax, at seventy-one, Kemp was impressive. A full head of grey hair was brushed tidily to one side. Slanting dark brown eyebrows stood out from his otherwise peaceful and friendly face. Six feet tall and 210 pounds, Kemp looked good in his loose-fitting black cardigan.

Kempton Hayes, left, and myself, 2005. Photograph by Andrew Safer.

"I can recall as far back as when I was five or six, and you were eight or nine," he began. "Do you remember when we found a pack of cigarettes on the railroad tracks, and you were going to show me how to smoke?"

We laughed at the memory.

"I had the cigarette in my mouth and I was blowing out," he said. "You told me to take a big suck in. So I did, and, suddenly, I couldn't breathe. So there I was, on the ground, choking, and gasping—and you were laughing!"

That same year, one afternoon Kemp was walking backwards in front of me as we headed over to his house from my place. We lived in the Armdale section of Halifax, near where the Armdale Rotary is today. In my right hand I was holding a flat board, narrowed at the end for gripping. I was batting stones. I'd pick up a stone about an inch in diameter, throw it up in the air, and bat it.

"Billy, cut that out!" Kempton said sharply. "You're going to hurt someone!"

I looked up and down the street. "How can I?" I replied. "There's no one around."

I struck another stone and instantly, Kemp fell over. He was wincing in pain and clutching his forehead. The gash was deep; blood was flowing onto the pavement. Crying and holding his head, Kemp ran the rest of the way home, and I followed.

Boy, did his mother ever chew me out!

Kemp pulled back his hair from the upper left side of his forehead, and said, "I don't know if you can still see the scar..."

While Kemp was recalling memories of the damage I had inflicted—or almost inflicted—on him, he recalled the time I was working for Eastern Photo Engravers (bookbinders and lithographic printers) when I was sixteen. I was cutting labels for Keith's India Pale Ale bottles. First, I'd position the die over a pad of paper, and then I'd turn on the big machine which sent a punch down, and the sharp edges of the die would cut the paper. Then I'd pick out the labels from inside the die, and go again.

I knew this was a dangerous piece of machinery because my buddy, Al Zinck, had mangled his finger while operating it a month before. (Years later, every time Al and I wrestled I was reminded of this.) Everyone was afraid of this machine.

On this particular workday, Kemp was hanging around watching.

"Put your hand in there," I told Kemp, just to see what he'd do.

He reached in and picked the die off the pad, his fingers curled over the top curve of the die. He figured the machine would automatically stop because his hand was there.

"Hey! Get your hand out of there," I yelled. He turned white as I told him that guys had had their hands crushed and their fingers cut off in that machine—because there was no safety mechanism.

To this day, Kemp wears Billy Taylor scars from the times I slashed his face with a hockey stick and mangled his thumb in the spokes of the front wheel of a tricycle.

After hearing him tell these stories, I had to ask, "Kemp, why did you put up with me?"

"Well, that time when you were batting stones and you hit me, I was mad but I wouldn't dare say it." Kemp looked me straight in the eye. "You were a tough guy."

That brought up another memory.

After a pause, he said: "You were my protector, Billy. Remember the local bullies? There were twenty-two in that family. I was scrawny. The average weight for my size was fifty-five, and I weighed forty-five. I wouldn't eat. They thought I had TB. But they were scared of you. You had quite a two-by-four on your shoulder from day one. Someone only had to look at you crossways and you'd beat on them. But you didn't do that to your close friends. Anyone who was picking on someone had to answer to Billy. You had to show how tough and independent you were because of your background."

"So it was protection? That's why you overlooked all these things?" I asked. It was news to me, after all these years.

"It wasn't only that. I always knew where you stood. You're as honest as anybody I know. If you said you're going to be somewhere, or do something, you were always there. You were the leader. It was all part of your persona of trying to be number one. You were compensating; you had a chip on your shoulder."

By the time Al Zinck and I wrestled that first pro match at the Shirley Street Arena, I had a reputation as a fighter. Kemp went away to college to become a doctor and I started learning the well-guarded secrets of the wrestling business.

3. WRESTLER

When I was eighteen, while I was working behind the Dominion Store meat counter on Quinpool Road in Halifax I met the woman who was to become my life partner.

Right away, I noticed Carol Anne Dauphinee's high cheekbones, auburn hair, peaches-and-cream complexion, well-shaped figure, and magnetic smile.

Over the next couple of weeks, Carol came back twice for hamburger, pork chops, and round steak. Each time, there was chemistry between us. I had never felt like this before! Finally, I got up the nerve to ask her name and phone number.

After stalling, she said "OK. My name is Carol and my number is in the book."

I was overwhelmed, as if I had just won a prize. After she took the parcels and left, I was bragging to the guys behind the counter when it hit me: I couldn't look up her number because she didn't give me her last name!

The next time Carol came in she was with her mother. When I passed Carol her usual meat order over the counter, she handed me a small folded piece of paper. I said good-bye and, expecting a love note, rushed into the cutting room to try to puzzle out what it said. (I could read letters but had a hard time putting them together into words.) Instead, I found myself staring blankly at a string of meaningless numbers. Then I realized she had given me her phone number!

We arranged to meet at six o'clock sharp for our first date. Her father answered the door. Irvin let me know straightaway that his fifteen-year-old daughter was not about to go out with an eighteen-year old man. (Carol had told me she was seventeen and I believed her because she seemed so mature.) Irvin told me to come back in six months when she turned sixteen, and shut the door in my face.

In the meantime, we went for long walks and sodas after school. Starting on Carol's sixteenth birthday, we went steady for about a year. Knowing that I was a professional wrestler, that I drank, and that I was "too old" for his daughter, Irvin didn't approve. A year later, he made a deal with a tenant who was a young cadet naval officer. Irvin would reduce his rent if this guy would steal Carol away from me. The old man's scheming worked—for a while.

I drowned my sorrows in beer. A few months later I was fired when I showed up for work stinking of alcohol. Soon afterwards I went to work at Eastern Photo Engravers, where I could get away with drinking on the job. (That was where I operated the die cutter that mangled Al's finger—the machine Kempton recalled some sixty years later.)

One day I came home from work and right there, standing in the front room, was Carol! She was giving my mother a permanent. We had not been on speaking terms but our tongues soon loosened up, and we got back together that evening.

When Carol was eighteen and I was almost twenty-two we decided to get married. Irvin, of course, wouldn't hear of it, so I found a way to go around him. Carol told me that her grandmother on her mother's side had a great deal of influence over her father. I became very good friends with Grandmother Pemberton and she came back with a "Yes", on the condition that we wait until Carol turned nineteen.

Irvin didn't say a word to me at the wedding.

Our wedding day (September 18th, 1955): Left to right:
Carol's parents: Marge and Irvin Dauphinee, myself,
Carol, my parents: Stan and Alice Taylor.
Photographer unknown.

We lived on the top floor of my parents' home in a one-bedroom apartment. Carol became pregnant six months after we were married and we named our first child Scott. Irvin and I had a couple of drinks which helped us bond on this happy occasion. At one-and-a-half year intervals Carol and I had three more children: Glenn, Steven, and Lynn.

Our children (much later): Left to right: Glenn, Steven, Lynn, Scott, 1962.
Photograph by Billy Taylor.

When Lynn was born, I was too drunk to be with Carol at the hospital. Our fifth and last child, Bill, was stillborn.

The day my innocent son died I blamed God: 'Is this just one more example of your handiwork?' I asked. Funny... It had never crossed my mind to thank him for the miracle of life when my four healthy children were born.

I always enjoyed babysitting the children when Carol went out shopping or to the hairdresser. The toddlers—bottles in hand—would giggle and laugh as they crawled everywhere in the house, and I'd be chasing after them—bottle in hand—giggling and carrying on. I think there should have been someone babysitting me.

As Carol used to say, "I raised five children: three sons, a daughter—and Billy."

It was 1950 and I had hit the big time. During my first week as a pro wrestler, a fan asked me for my autograph! My life had changed overnight. I had gone from loner to star—from stalling bill collectors to wrestling two matches a week for fifty dollars. And when I was paired up with name wrestlers that jumped to $200 or $250 a week!

Ringside seats were a dollar ten and children paid fifty-five cents admission. At twenty-five dollars a match, I was making top money for a pro wrestler—almost as much as my father brought home in a week. The cops or firemen who worked the full evening during a wrestling event only made three dollars.

I was the big cheese!

After one year in the business, I was getting paid $250 for matches in the cities—Halifax, Saint John, and Sydney—and I was also wrestling in the smaller outlying towns ("tank towns")—Berwick, Bridgewater, and New Glasgow. There were lots of opportunities in the tank towns because the big-name wrestlers didn't want to bother with them. A hundred dollars wasn't enough to interest them, but it was big money for me. As Len, the booker, explained, the money we earned in the tank towns would pay our (and his) expenses, and the bigger money in the cities was all gravy. Unlike the out-of-town wrestlers, I didn't have much in the way of expenses (motel, meals, and transportation) because I was living at home. So I took all I could get.

It wasn't long before my name was appearing on the list of matches in the Halifax newspaper. My brother, David, started to introduce me as "my brother Billy Taylor, the professional wrestling star."

I wanted to make sure my buddy Kempton knew what an important guy I was, so I sent him a photograph of Billy, the Big Time Wrestler. I had that mean look on my face that said, "Don't cross me, you sonofabitch". He knew it well!

Don't mess with Billy! Myself at 16, Canadian Forces
Base Stadacona, 1948. Photographer unknown.

After every match, a cooler of beer was waiting for the wrestlers in the dressing room. I always took a beer to show that I was "one of the boys", even though it tasted awful—compared to the orange juice I had trained on. But after the second beer I noticed that I would start to feel more sure of myself—in fact, downright cocky. I soon developed a drinking habit. What was strange is that booze never seemed to affect me. Only on rare occasions could others tell when I was half cut.

I always tried to win each time I went into the ring, even when I was pitted against well-known wrestlers. One night, I was standing in one of the Shirley Street Arena dressing rooms. It was a narrow room with a well-worn wooden bench and a shower head at the other end. Wrestlers were showering and getting dressed in the next room over. Suddenly, Len appeared.

"This may be a sport for some people," he said, "but for me, it's a business." He spoke in a quiet, businesslike tone. "And a very profitable business." At this point, he emphasized every word: "You will do as you're told in any match that you have. If you don't do as you're told and you want to be a hero, Billy, you can't work for me."

Then he added, "I'm not repeating myself. I hope I've made myself clear. Do you understand?"

"Yes," I replied.

Len patted me on the back and said, "Good boy, Billy, good boy."

From that moment on, I could only fight to win when that was the plan. I was a top-notch Roman Greco-style amateur wrestler, with the strength of two men, and it really pissed me off to let someone pin me to the centre of the ring when I knew I could beat him! I later took this up with Len, who sympathized with me and told me how I could get myself disqualified (DQ'd) instead, to save face.

I wasn't happy with this arrangement, but I wasn't dumb either. In those days, men didn't break into pro wrestling until they were in their late twenties. I had a ten-year jump on them. I had gone from carrying around a dollar or two in my pocket, to carrying around hundreds. I wasn't about to wreck a good thing.

Participating in fixed matches didn't bother me because I saw wrestling as entertainment. The fans were getting more than their money's worth with me, I figured. Besides, lots of things were fixed in the name of making a buck. The 1919 World Series was fixed and everyone knew it! I didn't see a problem.

The way it worked was that Len would tell us how the match was supposed to end before we went out into the ring—just like he did that first night—and then the wrestlers would communicate in code in the ring to keep things on track. "Put me over" meant to make me look good. "Don't throw potatoes" meant: don't hit me in the face with a closed fist. "We're going Broadway" meant: we'll wrestle to a draw. "The heat" referred to the cheering fans. "Let's go home" meant: it's time to end the match. "Develop a high spot" was: work the fans up to a pitch.

When wrestlers are talking about the business, or about how someone is to be handled, and a "mark" (non-wrestler) appears, someone will say "Kay Fabian" or "K-Fabe" to give the signal to change the conversation. If a person is "smart" it means he/she is in the know.

It took me about two months to learn the lingo.

There was one exception to the fixed matches: when two wrestlers had a beef and Len agreed to let them settle it in the ring. These disputes were usually over women or drugs. The fans didn't enjoy these real-life matches as much because they didn't last as long, and there was very little build-up before the action.

At about this time, the Halifax Police Department hired me as a part-time self-defense instructor. As I got to know some of the policemen, I began to imagine myself as a member of the force. The problem was, The minimum height was 5' 9". I was three inches too short.

I continued to teach amateur wrestling for about six years with the Halifax Police Boy's Club, and for about twenty years with the Halifax Police Rookie School and the Maritime Police School. I ended up teaching about 2,500 cops self-defense.

I was a self-defense instructor for the Maritime Police School and
Halifax Police Rookie School for 22 years (front, far right), 1963.
Courtesy Halifax Police Department.

As the years went by, Len became more than an employer to me, and I became more than a wrestler to him. In many ways, he was a father to me—more than my own dad—and I was his surrogate son. In 1952 I made a note in my diary of something Len's wife Kitty had told me: "Billy, Len always wanted a son," she confided. "One that he could be proud of. You know we never had any children. Len thinks of you as a son, so don't ever hurt him, please."

There's no question that Len gave me opportunities he didn't give the other wrestlers—opportunities to make it on my own as a pro. On my twenty-first birthday (1953) Len matched me with Jackie Nichols, the Junior Heavyweight Champion of the World. It was quite an honour! In a thirty-minute non-title match, Jackie let me "go Broadway" with him (wrestle to a draw), "putting me over" so I looked like a world-class wrestler.

After the match in the locker room I thanked Len, adding, "I appreciate this. I won't let you down."

Some years later, Jackie sent me a photograph of himself being honoured in a ceremony at the Maine Sports Hall of Fame. He had written across the front: "To my N.S. friend Billy Taylor, Canada's Finest Wrestler and Referee." I prized that photo like no other.

Jackie Nichols is being recognized here as an honorary member of the Maine Sports Hall of Fame, 1998.
Photographer unknown.

One day I was driving Len to a match in Sydney. Out of the blue, he asked, "Billy, would you be interested in doing a bit of shooting?" Shooting is a practice that is little known outside the profession. It's used to punish wrestlers who don't "cooperate" with the booker. If a wrestler fights to win after he's been told to lose (like I used to do before I knew better), he's a prime target for a shoot.

"We need to keep some of the newer, younger boys in line," Len explained.

After considering it for a few moments I replied, "No, I'm not interested."

Len pressed me further. "There'd be big bucks in it for you if you take on the job."

"How often would it be?"

"Just occasionally."

I was tempted by the money and wanted to please Len, so I said I'd do it.

My first assignment as a shooter was to teach a twenty-five-year-old newcomer a lesson. This guy wanted to beat everyone, and he wouldn't take "no" for an answer. I took him to the gym on the pretext that I might learn some moves from him, and he might learn something from me. Thirty seconds after I hooked him on the mat, he was on his stomach. I was sitting on top of him, using a step-over toe hold (my signature hold). I put my leg in the joint of his leg, and then sat on his leg. He cried out, "What the hell is going on, Billy?" Still sitting on him, I forced his arm behind his back and grabbed his wrist.

"You don't seem to want to listen and do as you're told," I said. "When you come back to see us next time, smarten up. Now, this is from Len, you fucker," and I broke his wrist.

He was rolling around the mat in agony, screaming. I got up and got dressed, picked up my suitcase, and walked out. He was out of commission for about a year. When he came back, he didn't work for Len.

I was paid $300 for that shoot. The ones that followed went up to $500.

My next shoot in Moncton took place during a match. The wrestler's mother, father, and girlfriend were in the audience, so instead of shooting I applied a leg lock and held it until the fellow hollered "I give up" at the top of his lungs—twice. Later I heard that he broke down crying in the dressing room because he had lost his first performance and was shamed in front of his loved ones. Len was furious with me for letting him off so easily.

With my brain soaked in alcohol and the big bucks coming in, it was easy to justify this sort of behaviour even though I found it difficult to look myself in the mirror. These people I was laming, possibly for the rest of their lives, were just like me when I started out: cocky and gunning to become a world champion in their first year.

The next time Len called on me to provide this service, I told him I wouldn't do it in front of an audience. We agreed the next shoot would take place at the Arena in the middle of the afternoon. Only Len and three Arena staffers were present. I brought the fellow in under the pretext of a work-out. As soon as we were on the mat I put the same leg lock on him that I had used in Moncton, except this time I went all the way and broke his leg. When I looked down, his leg bone was poking through his skin. There were bits of bone on the mat and blood on my tights and arms. I went over to the top rope and threw up on the Arena floor.

That was my last shoot.

Even though I saw shooting as part of the business, I was feeling guilty about maiming people for money. "I'm no better than some hoodlum," I told Len, "or a strong-armed bill collector who goes around collecting debts for loan sharks." Besides, I realized that if I continued to shoot, eventually one of these guys would fight back or get a friend to retaliate. Worse, I had met shooters who were a lot more vicious than me. I figured if I ever screwed up, one of them just might take care of me.

I had seen wrestlers put out of commission for good by shooters who would put the "stretch" on a guy. The wrestler would be lying on his stomach and the shooter would lay down on top of him, entwining their legs. Then he'd put a full nelson on the guy, and stretch until he tore everything that would separate—

hips, knee joints, neck, and shoulders. The poor bugger would never wrestle—and, in most cases, never walk—again.

I was too short to be a stretcher, and I sure as hell didn't want to ever end up on the receiving end.

When I told Len I was through shooting, he simply shrugged his shoulders and walked away.

As it turned out, the next generation of wrestlers didn't need to learn their lessons the hard way. They got the message that they were not going to become world champions right away, and that they had to abide by the rules of the wrestling business. That's why shooters became a dying breed. I was one of the last wrestlers to be recruited as a shooter in eastern Canada.

My unlimited capacity for booze lasted throughout my wrestling career, and well beyond. Once I got over my initial distaste for beer, I enjoyed it—particularly McEwan's Scotch Ale, which was about eight per cent alcohol. Three pints was enough to get a man drunk, but I would down six pints and go about my business as if nothing had happened. Including generous tips, I was spending about one-third of my income on booze.

At twenty-five, after I had been wrestling for seven years, I walked into the Arena one night and saw that my name wasn't on the cards. (Cards showed the line-ups of upcoming matches.) I went over to Len and asked when he would be needing me next.

"I can't use you anymore, Billy," he said matter-of-factly. "But if you're interested in a job as a referee, I'll give you all the work you want."

I was shocked. "I don't know what you're talking about, Len," I said. "Why can't I wrestle anymore?"

He paused for a moment and said, "The other wrestlers don't want to wrestle a drunk."

"I know I drink a bit at times," I said tentatively, "but I'm no drunk!"

This was unheard of. I didn't know there were any problems. About an hour later, Len approached me.

"Billy, I wouldn't call you a drunk either," he said, measuring his words. "But sometimes you're unpredictable. Listen, take my advice. Get out of the business, be a cop like you've always wanted to be, and get yourself sobered up."

The other wrestlers were afraid of me because sometimes I would move in and suddenly clamp down on them like a vise. I'd say, "Let's shoot!" I was only fooling around, but they didn't know it. I was using the ring as my place of power. Squared off on the mat, I was getting even for my growing-up years when people made fun of me because I was short and poor, and had no friends. But now it was backfiring on me. I was getting turfed from the profession that had treated me like a king!

I took Len's advice—except for the part about sobering up. I started refereeing, and my family pulled some strings to get me a job as a cop.

4. REFEREE

Jobs with the National Harbours Board were scarce, but a high-ranking politician owed my family a favour and a position opened up right away.

They hired me during my first interview! I had lived a stone's throw from the waterfront my whole life and knew everyone in the area, which probably helped. I would wear plainclothes and work as a trainee for six months. My second day on the job I was given an application to fill out. Thinking fast, I said I couldn't recall my wife's and children's birth dates. They told me to take it home and bring it back the next day.

Carol took care of the paperwork that night, which is when she began to teach me how to read and write. What saved me over the next six months was the fact that I didn't have to write any reports. By the time I put on a uniform and assumed the responsibilities of a harbour cop, I could read and write— enough to write a ticket, anyway. That same year, when I was twenty-five, Carol also taught me how to add and subtract.

I was soon proud of my reading ability. I sat my friend Fred down on the living room sofa and read aloud about "My Dog King" from a first-grade speller. In the story, the boy listed all of the things his police dog could do. When I finished, I closed the book and looked up at Fred, smiling. I expected him to cheer my newfound ability, but instead, he just sat there looking puzzled. Fred never knew I couldn't read. It was a closely guarded secret I had kept from everyone.

I started refereeing around the same time I started working at the Port, at twenty-five. I just had to juggle my schedule to make it work. My first matches as a referee were in Halifax, but then I travelled throughout Atlantic Canada, to Montreal, and down the eastern seaboard of the United States. I'd ref at night when I wasn't scheduled to work my beat on the waterfront. Because of my reputation as a shooter, I started off on the right foot. The wrestlers knew they couldn't push me around. During my thirty-year career as a ref I was only manhandled in the ring twice. Both times I took the offenders into the dressing room after the match and warned them that if they ever shot with me[2] again, I'd pin their shoulders to the mat and hold them there to a count—not to three, but to five hundred.

When a match was a "shoot", that means the wrestlers were going to fight for real. Someone was going to get hurt. There were only one or two shoots a year that took place in the ring either because someone was "throwing a potato" (hitting with a closed fist) over money, drugs, a girl, or gambling, or because of a disagreement over a title. Most shoots took place in the privacy of the dressing room.

The shoot between Bull (Doug) Curry and Joe (The Bat) Tomasso is one I'll never forget. Bull was the top drawing card and money-maker for this territory. Whatever Bull wanted, he got. Towards the end of Len's time as a promoter, Bull's son, Fred, showed up on the scene during his summer vacation from college.[2]

Fred changed the spelling of his last name (to Courie) to make it look like they weren't related. After Fred had been wrestling for about a month, Bull figured it was time he started "going over" (winning). Fred was going to be the hero, and Bull the villain. Fred's next match was with Joe (The Bat) Tomasso, a veteran wrestler. When I explained the finish to Joe, he said, "No fucking way is that young punk going over on me. Christ, Billy! What's Len thinking? The fans will never believe it."

Joe was right. Before this match, Len should have sent in a "carpenter" (a wrestler who builds up another wrestler in the ring, to make him look good to the fans), to set the stage.

When I told Len that Joe had refused, Bull piped up: "If Fred doesn't go over, I quit—right now."

Len turned to Joe and said, "Put Fred over or you're fired."

Eight or ten minutes into the match, Joe was lying flat on his back with his shoulders pinned. I counted one, two, three, and he got up and walked away as easily as if he had gotten up from his living room chair and walked across the room. Fred raised his arms in victory and the fans started booing and yelling, "Fake, fake!"

---

2 Shot with me: Here, "shoot" means to abuse the referee.

Bull had been watching every move in the ring. He was furious. He headed straight for Joe's dressing room for a "Hey rube[3]". It was the best fight of the night, and the fans missed it.

An unusual shoot involving two female wrestlers, thirty and eighteen years old, took place in Bridgewater in 1975. They had been on the circuit two weeks. One of the boys who had his eye on the young one picked her up and drove her to the match that night.

There were separate dressing rooms for the good guys (baby faces) and the bad guys (villains, or heels), and one room for the women. At about eight-thirty, the older girl, Dolly, ran into the dressing room and pointed a .22-calibre revolver at the guy who had brought Anna (the younger one).

"Stay away from Anna," she said in a husky voice. "If you go near her again I'll blow your fucking cock and balls off." With that, she left.

Out in the ring, I called the two of them to the centre for their instructions. The older one was glaring at the younger one, who was hanging her head as if she was being scolded by her mother. A minute into the match they started to shoot. Within thirty seconds Anna's eyes were black, her nose was almost broken, and her lip was split. She was lying on the mat in a fetal position, crying, while Dolly stood over her. If I hadn't been there, she would have started kicking Anna where it hurt, in the lower part of the stomach.

The fans were booing. They had paid good money to see two girls wrestle, and the match was over way too soon.

When I stepped between them to protect Anna, Dolly started to shove me and swear at me. I knew it wouldn't look good for me to be seen arguing with a woman in front of the crowd. If she and I hooked in the ring, it could start a riot. I squared off just a few inches from her and said, "Listen, don't start fucking with a shooter. If you do, when you go to your dressing room, I'll be there first and I'll kick the living shit out of you. If you don't think so, try me."

"I'm also a cop," I added. "And by the way, you'd better get rid of that heater[4] in your suitcase. Now, if you don't leave the ring I'll have the cops take you out." She threw me an ugly look, and left the ring. That was the end of it.

At about this time, I had a series of run-ins with Nature Boy Dillon. He was one of the best villains around—and he knew it. I'd walk into the dressing room and Dillon, this huge hulk, would be sitting on one of the benches smoking a cigar. I'd go up to shake his hand, and he'd just blow smoke at me. He never had any time for me. (Maybe he had something against drunks.)

---

3 This is the same as a bench-clearing in hockey or baseball, when two opposing team members get into a fight and then the rest of the players clear the benches and join them. In wrestling, the booker, promoter or another referee comes into the dressing room and hollers, "Hey, rube," and everyone goes to thoe ring to join the fight.
4 A "heater" is a gun.

One evening I was reffing a match between Dillon and Leo Burke. We were in the centre of the ring and Dillon was trying to intimidate me.

"Listen," I said. "Don't try to make *me* look bad or I'll DQ you."

"You stay the hell out of my way," he growled.

We went to our corners. Just before the bell rang, Burke came over to me and said, "Why not put my trunks on and go at Dillon right now, and I'll be the referee?" What he was really saying was, 'What the hell are you trying to do? You're the goddamn referee. Are you trying to put yourself over and make me look bad? Who's going to be the hero here?'

I got the message, and it saved the match.

A week later, I became a lot more involved in a shoot than I had planned. It was August sixth, 1975 and I was refereeing a five-bout card before a packed house at the Halifax Forum. There was a dull roar from the crowd, signalling their anticipation of a great match. I was in good spirits because I was looking at a few hundred dollar payoff.

Behind the scenes, Al, the promoter, was quiet and distant, which was unusual. Two of the top feature wrestlers, Leo Burke and Pierre LaSalle, couldn't show because they had both been injured in matches the night before. Substitute wrestlers would do their damnedest to fill their shoes.

In the semi-final match, Bulldog Bob Brown and Steve Bolas carried their fight outside the ring to the Forum floor. I had to step in and break it up because a spectator had been injured in a previous out-of-the-ring fight. Just before then, the Halifax Athletic Commission had told me: "Billy, if they fight outside the ring, stop the match by ringing the bell. If you don't, your license will be suspended."

I closed in on Brown to try to separate him from Bolas and he started to shoot with me, so I drove a right hand punch to the side of his jaw, and then DQ'ed him.

The next match was between Nature Boy Dillon from Florida and Johnny Weaver from North Carolina. Dillon and Brown were good friends, whereas I was good friends with Weaver.

I motioned Dillon and Weaver to the centre of the ring, said a few words, and then Dillon stepped forward so he was right in my face. "Taylor," he said. "Stay the hell away from me in this match." It was a fair warning, so I steered clear. Everything went OK until the third fall. Weaver was coming off the ropes as fast as he could, and Dillon pulled me right in front of him. Bam! It was like being hit by a five-ton truck. Down I went, clutching my sides in pain. I managed to signal that the match was over, and, for the sake of the fans, I DQ'ed Dillon (although that wasn't the proper finish).

Dillon came at me, throwing punches. He gave me a black eye and almost broke my nose. Realizing that a shoot was taking place, the wrestlers on the sidelines came to break it up. My good friend Rowdy "Rod" Piper helped me out of the ring and to my dressing room.

48 THE MAIL-STAR
Wednesday, August 6, 1975

Referee hero of wild bout

Referee Billy Taylor was the hero of the wrestling card at the Halifax Forum last night. He floored Bulldog Bob Brown with a right hand uppercut and withstood cruel punishment during the feature match between Nature Boy Dillon and Johnny Weaver, but kept his wits about him and saw enough going on to disqualify Dillon and hand the palm to Johnny Weaver.

Last night, Dillon attempted to do what no other wrestler could do and that was to pick up the $10,000 bounty placed on Weaver's head by Dillon. Dillon came no closer than the rest in achieving the goal.

Dillon took the first fall at 15.53 by applying two back crushers to the iron ringpost and elbow drop and two guillotines followed by a body press. Both men absorbed a lot of punishment during the 15 minutes.

Weaver evened the match at 6.06 with whips to the ropes and a sleeper that caused the referee to award the fall to Weaver. The end came at 4.44. Dillon whipped Weaver into the ropes and as he was coming off, Dillon pulled referee Taylor into the path of Weaver and both Weaver and Taylor crashed to the canvas. Dillon jumped to the top rope to pounce on Weaver, but Weaver slipped aside and Taylor awarded the fall and match to Weaver.

Dillon then proceeded to

The semi-final between Bulldog Brown and Steve Bolas was a rugged match all the way. Bolas took the opening fall at 13.42 after catching Brown in a spinning toe hold after whips to the ropes. Brown took the equalizer at 4.08 with karate chops, knee to the groin, a piledriver and a body press.

The end came at 2.52 when Brown whipped Bolas out through the ropes and then proceeded to give him a piledriver on the concrete floor. Referee Taylor jumped out of the ring and when Brown refused to let Bolas out of the hold, Taylor let go with a right hand punch that staggered Brown. Taylor then awarded the fall and match to Bolas.

In the special one fall tag team match, Mike The Judge Dubois and Lord Alfred Hayes defeated The Beast and Ron Thompson at the 9.57 mark when Dubois pinned Thompson with kicks to the face, and over the head neckcracker and a body press.

In the one fall single matches, Paul Peller defeated Frenchy Losier at 6.10 with knees to the stomach off the ropes, a leg lock and body press. In the opener, Rod Piper defeated Terry Yorkston at 7:27, with whips to the ropes, karate chops and his favorite finishing hold, the airplane spin and body press.

There were two substitutions on the card, all caused by previous injuries. Peller went in for Pierre LaSalle, Ron Thompson went in for Leo Burk.

It was announced from ringside that Mad Dog Martel would be featured on the card next Tuesday.

Republished with permission from The Halifax Herald Ltd.

In spite of this incident, outside the ring I've always had a lot of respect for Dillon who is a college graduate and a successful businessman.

Carol had been at the Forum that night and when we got home, she was close to tears. "For God's sake, Bill, give up this wrestling thing! It's not as though we need the money. I can't take the police job and the wrestling at the same time. Either one of them is bad enough for any wife. Please, stop!"

I knew it was tough for Carol, but I couldn't give either one up. I did quit refereeing—twelve years later.

The wrestlers knew I was a cop, but they did *not* know I was a self-defense instructor for the police, every one of whom was a shooter. In the self-defense course, I'd shoot with ten or twelve cops in each session, twice a week.

All this time I was working for Len, who had given me his east coast "territory". That meant that I reffed matches in the four Atlantic provinces over a twenty-five-week season (May to October). There was a pile of money to be made and I had been around long enough to know that if we gave the fans what they wanted, they'd be coming back for more, and Len would be happy. As he had told me on more than one occasion, "This may be a sport for some people, but for me it's a business. A very profitable business."

At the beginning of the season, Len would tell me what was planned for the entire twenty-five weeks: which wrestlers would appear, where and when; how each match would end (who would win and who would lose); and who would hold the various wrestling titles during the season.

Because I couldn't read or write most of my life, I had developed an exceptional memory. Since I couldn't write things down, I had to remember everything. Most wrestling referees could only remember one finish (the details of how one match should go). I could remember every finish for the whole wrestling card (five or six matches). On the days when I refereed one show at the Windsor Fair and another in Berwick that evening, I had ten finishes to remember!

It wasn't uncommon for a wrestler to forget his finish and ask me halfway through the match: "Ref, I forgot the finish! What do I do?"

"Grab him in a head lock and take him down," I'd say (for example) in a low voice so no one else could hear.

If the wrestlers were on the mat, I'd point my finger as if I was warning them about choking. What I was really saying was something like this: "When you get up, he'll throw you into the ropes. Come off with a tackle and knock him down. And then, a second tackle. This time, when he bends over, leap-frog him, and come off the ropes with another tackle. When he bends over, leap-frog over him, hook your legs under his armpits, and take him over in a sunset flip. I'll count one, two, three, you'll get up, and we'll go home."

Every Saturday night for three years I reffed televised matches across Atlantic Canada starring some of the biggest names in North American wrestling. In 1985 I reffed the match between Jack Brisco from the United States, the Heavyweight Champion of the World, and Leo Burke from Dorchester, New Brunswick. Other matches featured Whipper Billy Watson, The Bulls (Montana and Curry), Freddie Sweettan, Lou Thesz, Gene Kiniski, Andre "The Giant",

"The Beast" (Ivan Cormier), "Killer" Karl Krupe, and Bulldog Brower. I reffed on the same cards as hockey great Maurice "The Rocket" Richard, and world boxing champs Jack Dempsey and Joe Louis. I also reffed some well-known boxers like Yvon Durrelle, twice contender for the light heavyweight champion of the world.

(Photo on Left) Myself (left), Yvon Durelle (right), Baie-Sainte-Anne, New Brunswick, 1998. I'm wearing the boxing gloves Yvon wore when he fought Archie Moore for the world's light heavyweight championship in 1958. Photograph by Freda Atkinson.

(Photo on Right) I was refereeing this match Bull Montana (left) and Yvon Durelle (right), circa 1978. Photograph by O. J. 'Ossie' Timmins.

Bulldog (Dick) Brower was a major attraction in the Maritimes. After seeing him wrestle in a Toronto match on TV, I told Len I thought he'd go over well in our neck of the woods. Many years of weightlifting had made him a very stocky and powerful man. At about 5' 10", Bulldog weighed close to 300 pounds, and every one of those pounds was well-proportioned—unlike a lot of the other wrestlers who were bulked up on top, but had no legs.

A big crowd turned out to watch Bulldog's first match in Halifax. As he walked from the dressing room to the ring, what struck me was the puzzled look on his pudgy face. His lips were drawn tight; something was clearly bothering him. He kept hunching his right shoulder, and, every now and again, he'd twist his neck to the right and look up at the ceiling for no apparent reason. As he approached the ring, he banged his forehead on the ring buckle to show his anger.

By now, the fans were booing. Bulldog was known as a raving lunatic; that's why he was such a good draw. By this time he had risen through the ranks of weightlifting competitions to become the fourth strongest man in the world.

Whenever things weren't going his way in the match, he'd jump outside, bang his head on the ring apron, and, hunching his shoulder, look up at the ceiling before jumping back into the ring.

As referee, I was nervous because with Bulldog, I never knew what was coming. Soon, I'd be looking up at the ceiling and telling myself, 'I'm getting as crazy as he is!'

During his first week in the Maritime circuit, I picked up Bulldog and Len one evening and drove them to Berwick. That was when I learned the truth about this "madman".

Dick Brower always did very well in school. His family was well off and he was college educated. He told me he worked with people with mental disorders, learned their mannerisms, and acted them out in the ring! Everyone was calling him a nutcase because of the idiotic things he did. Little did they know that he was having the last laugh!

This wasn't a complete surprise because I'd known many fakes in the business. There was an Indian who used to do a war dance wearing war feathers, who was really a guy from a wealthy Jewish family in the southern US. Then there was a Japanese wrestler who used to bow, clasp his hands together, and say "Ahso". Out of respect, I'd bow to him...until one day I realized he was saying "Asshole!"

We used to play a lot of jokes on each other. One night at the Halifax Forum, Andre the Giant (who was 7' 4", weighed 475 pounds, and wore a size 22 shoe) was going to wrestle two villains. The booker took me aside before the match and told me the plan. I was to make small talk with them in the centre of the ring and tell them to go to their corners, but I would turn around and go to my corner first. That's when the villains would run after Andre and pound him before the bell rang. The match wasn't supposed to start until they got in those free punches.

After giving them their instructions in the centre of the ring, I sent them to their corners, but as I started to turn around, Andre was standing on my right foot. The two villains just stood there and stared at me, as if to say, "Do something!" Finally, one of them blurted out, "If you don't go to your corner, you're going to screw this up for us." Meanwhile, it felt like a six-inch spike had nailed my sneaker to the floor. This went on for about a minute while the fans were getting more and more restless for the match to start. There wasn't anything I could do. Finally, Andre had enough of the joke. When he got off my foot, I realized he had been in on the game of making me look stupid. I headed for my corner and everything else went according to plan.

One night, I opened my wrestling bag in the dressing room to change my shoes. It was ten minutes before the match, and my wrestling shoes weren't there! I phoned Carol to send a spare pair by taxi, but there was no way they would arrive in time.

"I bought a pair of sneakers for my son today," Leo Burke said in a friendly voice. "They don't look exactly right, Billy, but they'd be better than going out in your sock feet. You're welcome to wear them." He held up a pair of red sneakers. One said "Donald Duck" and the other said "Mickey Mouse". I didn't have a choice, so I put them on and went into the ring for the nine o'clock start. It was a big match, and the Forum was packed. They announced the wrestlers. Leo took one look at my shoes, and busted up laughing. The other guy did the same, and soon he was hanging onto the ropes for support. Next it spread to the timekeeper, and then to the fans. Over 6,000 people were laughing at me! As soon as the match was over, I stormed out of the ring—and they were still laughing!

In the dressing room, I told the guys that I quit. And then I noticed my sneakers sitting on the bench. 'OK, so that's why Jim sidetracked me as soon as I got here tonight,' I told myself, piecing together the story. 'He was confiding in me about a problem at home so the other guys could set me up. That gave Leo a chance to swipe my sneakers and put them in his suitcase.'

For two weeks after that, wrestlers would take one look at me and crack up, remembering me in those red sneakers. About a month later, after it had blown over, I got even with Leo. I took the shoelaces out of his sneakers and no one would lend him a pair. I finally let him use a pair of pink laces I had brought with me for the occasion.

Without playing these jokes on each other, it would have been like any other job—boring!

Years later, Kempton told me: "Billy, you were the first of the big time WWF actors. You really had the role down. You knew when to fall, when to stop counting, when to give somebody hell, and when to get clipped. But that white shirt didn't do anything for your gut."

"That's what I *wanted* people to think," I explained. "That was part of my plan." Fans would holler at me, 'Your gut's hanging out! Get some exercise!' I wanted them to get pissed off with me because I couldn't get down fast enough to count, or I had trouble getting up from the ring. In reality, I could have moved faster than most of the wrestlers, but I liked tormenting the fans. I'd rub my eyes and squint to make it look like I couldn't see, and then look in the wrong corner. I'd count the good guys fast, and the bad guys slow. Sometimes, I'd forget the count and start over. It was all part of the show.

All of the matches were staged to manipulate the fans—and bait them for more. In a "work", the wrestlers grab each another gently, as if they're handling eggs. In a "shoot", they mean business and someone is going to get hurt. In a "friendly shoot", they wrestle to win but no one gets hurt.

One of my favourite matches was a friendly shoot between Lou Thesz, a seven-time winner of the heavyweight champion of the world title, and North American Heavyweight Champion Leo Burke. It was at the Halifax Forum in

1982. All 7,000 seats were taken. The promoter had arranged that they would each take a fall, and then the third and final fall was up to them.

On the last fall, Thesz had Burke down. His shoulders were just barely off the mat. Straining to pin Burke, Thesz shouted at me: "For God sake's ref, count him out!"

"I can't count him out," I said in a voice the fans couldn't hear.

"Why not?"

"Before the match I bet fifty dollars with one of the boys that Burke would win."

Thesz let go of Burke and busted up laughing.

"Thesz," I said, "you give me $200 and I'll disqualify this sonofabitch and we'll both make money." By this time he was hysterical. Thesz was begging me to stop. As it turned out, he won the match. On the way out of the ring I turned to him and said, "I'll never ref you again. I'm losing money on you!"

Of course, that wasn't true! For that match I was paid the equivalent of a week's salary—not bad money back in 1982.

When I reffed the Midget Wrestlers in Newfoundland I'd wind up lying on the ring mat laughing so hard I couldn't get up. There was no planned finish with Little Beaver, Sky Lo Lo, Tom Thumb, and Cowboy Carlson, who always wrestled tag team. None of them knew how it was supposed to end. First, they would all pile on top of me and tie my boot laces together so when I stood up I'd trip and fall. Then they would pile on top of me again and Beaver would count down: one, two, three, and all four of them would raise their arms as winners, hamming it up for the crowd.

One time these little sneaks managed to slip off my belt without me noticing, so that as soon as I took a step, my pants fell down. And I was being paid top money for this!

After I had reffed for a few years, Len initiated me into another secret practice of the trade: blade running. A blade runner skillfully uses a tiny piece of razor blade embedded in a Band-Aid on his index finger to intentionally cut one of the wrestlers during a match. This was used to create a display of bloodshed, in order to work up the fans and whet their appetite for a rematch. Only certain referees are entrusted with this honour.

One day, Len approached me in an out-of-town dressing room.

"Billy, when some of the wrestlers use their own blades to cut themselves to draw blood, they look too obvious," he confided. "Besides, I worry about one of these wrestlers misplacing his blade. I'm afraid someone in the audience is going to find it. We have to keep this to ourselves."

I waited, because I knew more was coming.

"Would you like to handle the blade, Billy?"

Daily News, Friday, December 28, 1984

LEN HUGHES, ONE OF MY EARLY HEROES, PASSES ON

Al Hollingsworth

THERE WAS A TIME when wrestling was one of the most popular sports in metro. Especially in the days before TV.

The old Shirley Street Arena would be packed to the rafters to see some of the best in the world perform. Among them was everyone's favorite, Len "Cowboy" Hughes. He was truly a hero among local sports fans.

In those days, wrestling was treated as a legitimate sport. Newspapers and radio stations gave them equal time. And when Len Hughes came to town there was a little extra hype given the matches.

I can recall the sports columnists, Alex Nickerson and Ace Foley, covering the matches and writing glowing pieces about the men inside the ropes. Len Hughes was one of their favorites too.

The advent of television and the proliferation of the sport on the tube kept people away from the matches and the sport saw a marked decline in attendance. Many wrestlers hung up the trunks in despair.

Not Len Hughes. He continued for years, moving with the promoters to the Forum when the Arena fell victim to the hammer.

And while he made a comfortable living from the sport, he took time to give something back. Many young wrestlers got their start under his eye. Several local wrestlers got their start from him. Al Zinck, who later became a promoter, was one of his pupils. So too were Ozzie Timmons and Billy Taylor. They later traded the trunks for referee jerseys.

Visiting wrestlers were quick to ask of his whereabouts, his state of health. I recall a couple of years ago, having a private chat with Bulldog Bob Brown. "How's Len Hughes, where is he living?" was the first words he said after we shook hands.

"How about driving me out to see him one of these days?" he suggested.

Sadly, we never made the trip.

Hughes, a native of Mount Cisco, New York, not only liked the reception he received here, he liked the area. So much so, that when he retired he made Nova Scotia his home.

In recent years he lived in Allen Heights until failing health had him go to Shoreham Village in Chester.

Wednesday, a 15-line account of his death was carried at the bottom of page 35 in the Chronicle-Herald. Len Hughes had passed away on Monday at the age of 76.

And while he is gone from our midst, those of us who shared his corner for so many, many years, will never forget the pleasure he brought to our lives.

My friend Al Hollingsworth wrote this column to commemorate Len's passing.
The Daily News, December 28, 1984.
Reprinted with permission from Al Hollingsworth.

57

Without hesitating, I said yes. There was no more money in blade running, but I knew it would enhance my position as a referee who could be counted on for important assignments.

From that time on I was called upon to perform this service about twice a year for the rest of the time I was refereeing. One day, out of the blue, Carol asked me, "Billy, who is the Blade Runner?" She had heard references to this secret practice, but I never said a word.

If you look at a close-up photo of a wrestling star from the 1950s, 1960s, or 1970s, you'll probably see a lot of scars on his forehead—and nowhere else on his face. That's because the refs would us the blade just above the eyebrows. The ref would move in as if to separate the wrestlers, but he was really landing a well-placed slice just above the eyebrow of the chosen wrestler. I'd generally use the blade in a taped-fist match, when the wrestlers' fists were wrapped with white tape, and punches were allowed. After the slice, the aggressor would pound on the "victim's" forehead until he bled.

Not long after that, Len died of cancer and it felt as though something in me had died—something I could never replace. I was so upset I couldn't bring myself to attend his funeral.

In 1987, I was refereeing a match in Bridgewater. In this "chain match", the wrestlers were joined by a ten-foot heavy chain that was hooked to a leather strap around their wrists. It impresses the fans when one of them puts the chain around the other's neck as if to choke him, winds it around his feet, or ties him up while stomping on him. The fans were primed because the wrestlers were scheduled to come back the following week for a no-holds-barred, fight-to-the-finish, no-time-limit match. I was supposed to cut one of the wrestlers during the last of five matches. This would kill the action so the promoter could bring them back for a rematch. A cut fighter remains in the running, whereas if he's KO'd (knocked out), that kills the action.

I had been drinking heavily that day. During the intermission before the semi-final match, I placed a one-eighth-inch triangular razor blade fragment under my Band Aided finger, and in the third fall of that match, I cut Sam. As the blood spurted from his forehead, I stood in the corner of the ring smiling at what a good job I had done. Better than a surgeon! Meanwhile, Sam and his opponent were standing in the centre of the ring, dumbfounded. They finished the match with a submission hold. Sam immediately went into convulsions.

Sam's two brothers rushed him to the hospital's emergency room where he was saved from bleeding to death.

I had severed an artery on his temple instead of nicking the skin above his eyebrow—but, thanks to the booze, I hadn't noticed.

In the dressing room, the promoter was pacing and shaking his head in disbelief. He gestured at me when I walked in. "Why, Billy? Why?" he asked, distraught. "Why didn't you follow your instructions?" His face showed utter disgust.

"We can't cut another wrestler tonight," he went on. "Now next week is all screwed up! Billy, you should drink *after* the match, not *before*. Everyone would be a hell of a lot better off."

I still didn't know what was wrong. "I only did what you said," I managed, as I started to get undressed to go home.

"Where the fuck do you think you're going?" he shouted.

Then it hit me. This was only the third match! Boy, had I screwed up! I had cut the wrong man, thinking it was the feature (or last) match. (Later, I found out how close the wrestler came to dying.)

Immediately, I started rationalizing. Someone must have told me wrong. It wasn't my fault. I don't make mistakes. I'm the best in the business.

The promoter interrupted my train of thought. "Billy," he said, "we can't continue with you anymore." We had known each other since we were wet-behind-the-ears wrestler wannabes. "I think it's time you looked at retiring from this business. If this continues, and you ever do cut the wrong man again, he just may be a better shooter than you. The shoot would take place after the match in the dressing room."

I was in shock—and totally fed up with myself. I wondered what in the hell was wrong with me. What was I going to do now?

We did the feature match "without the juice"[5]. As for Sam, they stitched him up and he walked out of the hospital that night. I showered and went home, but didn't sleep. The next morning I took my referee clothing, wrestling boots, and tights into the backyard, poured stove oil on them, and lit a bonfire. I watched my thirty-seven year career in the wrestling business—which had been very good to me—go up in thick black smoke.

Sam had been a good friend, but we dropped out of touch soon after that match. Five years later I ran into him in a coffee shop in Truro. All along, he thought the chain had cut him. When I told him the real story, he shrugged it off, saying, "That sort of thing is bound to happen in the wrestling business sooner or later."

You won't see much blade running today because of the scare of AIDS. One of the last feature juice matches I reffed back in 1986 was in Bridgewater. When Leo Burke stepped into the ring, there was blood all over the mat from a nosebleed in the previous match. He looked up and said, "Billy, I hope this guy doesn't have AIDS." That made me leery because a lot of times I would end up on the mat after someone had been bleeding.

There were several factors that helped destroy wrestling in the Maritimes: overexposure on TV, poor showmanship, drugs, and booze. Len had quit the

---

5 Without bloodshed. A feature juice match has plenty of blood.

promotion business in the late 1960s, largely because of wrestlers like me who had no respect for the fans who were paying our salaries. I always drank before I entered the ring, and I couldn't wait for the match to be over so I could keep drinking.

Today's wrestling bears little resemblance to the wrestling I knew. There used to be a science to applying a hold, using a counter hold and escaping from a hold. Now it's mostly kicking, punching, and theatrics.

When I was in the ring—either wrestling or refereeing—any wrestler who jumped off the top rope onto his opponent was immediately disqualified and in some cases the Athletic Commission would fine him $200. Today, if they could go to the top of the arena and jump off the roof, they would.

The only time we could use a closed fist was in a taped-fist match, and hair-pulling was not allowed. Now, "wrestlers" can do just about anything except hit each other over the head with a two-by-four—and that's probably coming. Today, "professional wrestling schools" teach every kid and his dog to be a pro wrestler. What these kids don't realize is that to make it as a pro, you need at least five years' experience as a competitive Roman Greco amateur-style wrestler, three to four years of bulk weightlifting three times a week, and you need to run five to six miles or bike twenty-five miles a day. Combined with mat workouts and weightlifting, this gives the wrestler both the wind endurance and the staying power he needs to hold his own against a shooter, not to mention an old-fashioned street fighter. I started this training as a young teenager and kept it up the whole time I was wrestling. Since I was short, I needed to develop muscle mass and endurance so I could face these guys and wrestle them on my terms.

Kids who believe wrestling is a game find out the hard way when a good amateur teaches them a lesson by breaking their wrist or leg, or worse.

And what about steroids? People like Lyle Alzado, the famous football star, get as big as two doors. Lyle died from brain cancer at the age of forty-three.

There's less shooting now than in my time. Wrestlers don't act on their own so much anymore because the sport has become like a circus sideshow, with greater bucks to be had for those who don't rock the boat.

Wrestling is now a glorified entertainment bonanza. When I started out in the ring, Gorgeous George Wagner was the only "character", followed by Nature Boy Buddy Rogers. Then came the villains—the Japanese, Germans, and Russians (who were actually Canadians and Americans). Today, just about everyone is wearing a costume. They dance around the ring like elves, and sometimes they twirl around like ballerinas. I haven't watched a wrestling match, either live or on TV, for over ten years.

5. WATERFRONT COP

On January 8, 1958 I was hired to work as a constable at the Port of Halifax—where I wasn't too short, and where you didn't have to read and write to get a job.

Right away, I ran into a friend who had been working there for years. I had known one-time boxer Clarence Bayers from my mother and father-in-law's home. He wasted no time in cluing me in about the waterfront.

"Now, don't be too gung ho and try to arrest anyone," Clary cautioned, "because the waterfront is not actually run by port officials. It's controlled by the Longshoremen's Union. Whatever the president of the union wants, he gets." Clary looked me in the eye. "And I'm talking about the man at the top in the union's New York City office."

What Clary said stayed with me.

He said I was expected to turn a blind eye to the theft of cargo on the shipping end of things, and the same held true for theft at the Port's cold storage plant and the grain elevator. I could either make it easy for myself, or I could get myself into a lot of hot water. A lot of cops were looking the other way, and if I was smart, I'd do the same.

I stored Clary's words in the back of my mind, and kept my eyes open. I had no idea that thirty years later I would say to myself, "Clary, you sonofabitch, you knew what you were talking about. You were right on the money, only it was a lot worse than what you told me that day."

After the winter shipping season, in April, nine cargo-carrying steamships were berthed at vacant piers between Pier 9 (Richmond Terminal) and Pier 31

(Ocean Terminals). These Canadian National steamships were there because the Seafarer's International Union was on strike.

The federal government which owned the steamships hired watchmen from the International Longshoremen's Union to keep an eye on the ships' furniture, tools, and equipment.

Sometimes when I was walking my beat I'd board the ships and make small talk with the watchmen. There was only one on duty at a time. Eighteen watchmen were on rotation. They were men in their sixties who had come out of retirement for this job.

After a few weeks, one of them told me: "Billy, there was stuff coming off the ships through the motorboat service when the ships were anchored in the harbour."

I began to notice a difference in the activity on the piers in the daytime, and at night. In the early hours of the morning, a half-ton truck would pull up. Large boxes, chairs, tables, and other items were loaded, and the truck would drive away.

I was puzzled because there was always a watchman guarding each ship. One day, one of the other cops brought it up. "Don't worry about it, Billy," he said. "Everything's all right!" That seemed odd!

A couple of the night watchmen told me I could have anything I wanted—dishes, furniture, you name it. I just had to say the word. I figured they were setting me up. If I went along with it, I wouldn't be able to say anything.

Over the next couple of months, the night traffic increased at the piers. Instead of one vehicle, there were two, and then three.

When I boarded the ships, I started to notice that chairs, desks, and tables that had been there, were gone. It was particularly obvious on the ship that was berthed at Pier 9, which was an out-of-the-way spot. I boarded it once a week and each time it looked emptier.

After the first two or three months, I suspected that the ships were being robbed blind. I finally went to talk to a port official. "Keep your eyes closed and your mouth shut," he said. "And don't forget—you're still on probation."

I wanted the job, so I backed off.

This went on for almost a year. There was no heat on the ships, the engines were idle, and everything was corroded. A couple of them had started to list and were taking on water.

The ships were finally sold to the Cuban government for scrap, and were towed out of the harbour. By this time, there was very little left onboard—even the brass and copper fittings were gone!

Soon after they left, I learned that some of the port officials, a shipping company representative, and quite a few cops had been in on it.

A few months later I was doing a visual search of an elderly stevedore's vehicle because I didn't have the authority to check bags and parcels.

"Before you check people like me," he said, "why don't you check your own people?"

"You mean the cops?" I asked. I didn't know where this was going.

"Yeah. What did you get off the ships?"

"What do you mean?"

"You know what went missing. Pretty well everything. The cops got their kickbacks. Didn't you get yours?"

No one accuses *me* of theft. I came unglued, and gave him an earful.

"You're probably the only one that's not in on it," he said.

I later found out that the port official who told me to play deaf and dumb had installed two gas tanks in the trunk of his car, which were connected to his main tank. That way, when he filled up at the National Harbours Board garage, he filled the extra two tanks while he was at it. He never had to pay for gas.

As soon as it was obvious that the steamships wouldn't be leaving the harbour, the crooks must have spotted the opportunity. "Sharing the wealth" was their MO for making sure no one squealed.

But then I figured maybe the federal government just let the ships go to hell—so they wouldn't have to deal with the union.

As a trainee, I had gotten to know the manager of National Sea Products' fish processing plant. Like a lot of waterfront workers, he knew me from my wrestling days. Ralph told me that shortages at the plant the previous year had cost the company $30,000.

During the fishing season, two trawlers landed approximately 300,000 pounds of fish every day. So who would miss it if each plant worker stole two or three measly pounds?

The fish was first weighed when it was unloaded, it was processed, and then it was weighed again before being placed in the cold storage plant. (The only facility of its kind in Nova Scotia, the plant was used to store imported and local poultry, pork, lamb, and beef for the local food chains.) Ralph figured the plant workers had to be involved in the scam because the before and after weights rarely tallied. On this particular Wednesday I stopped the workers as they were heading home. They were allowed to take home one or two pounds each week, but I was finding five and six pounds per person in each car.

I caught one wiry worker with twelve pounds of haddock fillets. I seized them and told him he would be charged with theft by way of a summons. Then I marked the parcel so it could be identified in court and placed it in the freezer compartment of the cold storage plant. The plant foreman had told me I had the only key to that padlock.

A half hour later, two fish plant workers pulled up to the police station. One of them—a tall, thin man in his late thirties wearing a red checkered hunting shirt and a brown cap—called out to me: "Officer, can I speak to you outside?"

As I walked up to his car, he said, "If you overlook this incident of extra fish from the plant, there's a five-gallon bucket of scallops waiting for you." He was pointing to the trunk of his car.

"I have no intention of dropping any charges or turning the fish back over to you. And you'd better watch yourself or you'll be charged with obstructing justice and bribing a police officer."

The fellow's face turned serious and he shot back: "If you don't play ball, you're not only jeopardizing the plant workers who get extra fish. Don't forget that the cops always get their weekly supply too. You'd better be careful whose toes you step on."

If he thought he could buy me, he had another thing coming. I took after my Grandmother Susan. Granddad had learned how to make shoes in prison, and when he was released from Dorchester, he opened his own shoe business in New Glasgow which turned out to be quite a successful enterprise. Many years after deserting her, Granddad wanted to share his wealth with Grandma and the children—but he was too late. She showed him the door without a second thought. I've always admired Grandma for that.

Two days later I received an anonymous phone call from someone suggesting I check on my evidence. I went to the cold storage plant and the haddock fillets were gone. So there *was* another key!

I had no choice but to drop the charges.

Ralph wasn't surprised when I told him about the disappearance. He went on to tell me about some major shortages at the plant since he had started working there.

One steel grey day a merchant ship full of whole, gutted pigs was waiting to be unloaded. I had been on the job about eight months, and was called down to patrol the brow. (The brow is the strip of pavement between the moored ship and the storage shed where cargo is unloaded.) The pigs were scheduled to be unloaded and extra port cops were on duty to keep an eye out for theft. The cargo was to be moved from a refrigeration ship onto flatbed trucks on the brow at Pier 26, and then hauled in for cold storage.

Five eighteen-man gangs of stevedores were working that shift, and Don was the gang boss that day. He stood 6'2" and I figure he weighed a trim 175 pounds. Don's cotton hook was hanging from his web belt. He signalled to a few stevedores on board the refrigeration ship, and they headed down the gangway. Partway down, one guy said to his buddy in the middle: "You'll be OK, Pete," and then he started to sing a tune. A little over five feet tall, the one in the middle was dressed in a greatcoat, black work boots, and glasses. He had a pipe in his mouth, and a black woollen cap was pulled down over his glasses. I noticed his feet weren't touching the ground. Just then, Don approached one of the other harbour cops and said, "Pete here had too much to drink last night. I'm going to call a taxi to take him home."

"Good idea," the cop replied.

A couple of minutes later, a taxi pulled up. The two stevedores hefted their drunken buddy onto the backseat and laid him out flat.

"Sleep it off, Pete, until you get home," one of them called out as the taxi drove off.

A few days later I heard that one of the hogs had gone missing from that ship. With so many cops on duty that afternoon, I couldn't see any possible way that could have happened. Soon after, a longshoreman walked up to me with a devil-may-care look on his face. "I hear you've been invited out to a lovely pork roast dinner at the home of one of the boys who was working on the hog ship," he said.

That "drunk" the taxi carted off was "Pete" the Pig!

The waterfront thieves were brazen—and crafty. Being on the look-out all the time wasn't enough. I had to think as creatively as they did.

From my first day on the job, one thing separated me from the other cops. I had proven that I was tough both in the wrestling ring, and as a self-defense instructor. Not only did people think twice before crossing me, but I wasn't afraid of anyone because I knew I'd win in a physical confrontation. I had taught the four types of force[6] at the Maritime Police School and to the Port Police, and a lot of people on the waterfront knew that I knew.

I had been on the job about a year when I was called to a disturbance on a cargo ship at Pier 22. On deck, things seemed to have settled down so I had a couple of shots of rum with the Chief Mate. As I was leaving, Big Mac was hollering at the stevedores. He was a Customs officer with thirty-four-and-a-half years' service—just six months to go before he could claim his pension. At 6'3" and 260 pounds, Big Mac was an imposing man. When he was drunk, he would sucker punch people for no apparent reason. Everyone on the waterfront was afraid of him because he was such an unpredictable and pigheaded bully.

He had a lot of alcohol in him this particular afternoon, and he was a holy terror. He stood there on deck with a look of violence on his face—clenched fists at his sides, eyes piercing. One of the older stevedores on deck, Clary Soward, was the winch man. Coming out of nowhere, Big Mac punched Clary

---

6. Police officers use four types of force:
1. Oral: The officer's tone of voice and words spoken should be polite, yet firm, and businesslike.
2. Touch: The officer places his hand on a person in a firm, easy manner.
3. Non-deadly force: Police holds and come-alongs are used when an officer needs to lead someone away against his or her will. The hold exerts physical pain, but it doesn't inflict injury.
4. Deadly force: This force is used to kill. When resorting to deadly force, the officer must keep in mind Sections 25 and 26 of the Criminal Code. To paraphrase Section 25, any peace officer or anyone who is aiding a peace officer may use as much force as is necessary in order to administer or enforce the law as long as that person acts "on reasonable grounds." Further, Section 26 states that we can be held criminally responsible for "any excess thereof."

in the face and broke his glasses. The winch let loose and dropped wildly into the ship's hold.

Just as the stevedores were about to turn on Big Mac, I stepped in and threw him to the deck of the ship, put my step-over toe hold on him, forced his hands behind his back, and handcuffed him. With the help of a couple of longshoremen, I stood him up, threw him over my shoulder, and carried him down the gangway. A waiting police car drove him to the station.

The Big Mac story was soon common knowledge since word travels fast on the waterfront. He had helped me establish my reputation.

When I was in the force there was no written Code of Conduct to discourage cops from manhandling troublemakers, other than what was written in the Criminal Code, so I was free to use my wrestling skills on the job. Nowadays, cops have to be extremely careful when they use physical force to restrain someone, and the days are long gone when a cop could apply a step-over toehold!

Big Mac was terminated from his position with Canada Customs and he lost his entire pension.

During my first five years as a harbour cop, a good many of the cops could not resist a bribe, so I learned to play it cool. Without back-up, I couldn't act on a lot of the crime that was happening on my beat.

The salary that most police forces in the 1950s and 1960s paid wasn't a respectable living wage. When I started out, my annual salary was a whopping $2,780, with my work clothes thrown into the bargain. After one year I was given a $600 raise, to just under $3,400 a year.

Luckily, I wasn't relying solely on my income from the National Harbours Board because my second career of refereeing was much more lucrative. I could afford to stay honest! These first years, when I didn't have any back-up, I concentrated more on my other profession. On the waterfront—for the most part—I steered clear of trouble.

Around this time, Denny came to work on the force. When we met, we didn't get along. Denny walked into the Pier 25 precinct office and asked if I had seen the topcoat he had left behind the night before. His tone of voice was disrespectful, and I didn't like the offhanded way he said "Hey, b'ye".

"No, why ask me?" I replied. "Do you think I took it? I don't wear kids' clothing."

We had a few angry words and wound up giving each other a wide berth for the next year or so. During that time, I could tell he was an honest cop. Even though we didn't get along, I wanted to partner with him but it took a few years for us to trust each other enough to start working together.

At that time I was planning to quit the force. I figured I could make bigger money wrestling, get away from shift work, and leave a job where I was hopelessly outnumbered. Unlike many others, I had been turning down a bribe a month, on average. The week I decided to submit my resignation, Captain

Gatheny, a wrestling fan who was a high-ranking shipping official, told me I should stay because the waterfront police were in for some big changes. He couldn't tell me any more, but I knew I could trust him so I stayed on another year.

I'm glad I did.

It wasn't long after Captain Gatheny tipped me off that four other port cops and I were promoted to sergeant.

Photograph by Lysia Taylor.

The powers that be passed over the older members, forcing them into retirement. This sort of treatment was unheard of back then. It was the first sign of changes to come. When the senior men went in to discuss their pensions with management, they were told about "a possible reorganization".

The next thing I knew, George Brennan, the manager of the cold storage plant, was promoted to the new office of Police Administrator. His job was to oversee the daily operations of the Port Police. The sergeants would report to him, and he would report to the Port Manager.

At first, I was cynical about Brennan because of what I'd been through with theft at the cold storage plant. I figured if he couldn't keep things under control at one relatively small operation, how in the hell was he going to handle the whole port? But I was glad to see him in that role because anything would be better than having to work under the Deputy Chief. Even so, I didn't believe that anyone could make a difference at the Port, so I figured I'd just watch from the sidelines.

Brennan's first test came soon. Over 100 workers from the National Harbours Board Labour, Water, and Electrical Departments set up a picket line at the grain elevator. Poultry farmers from around the province depended on daily grain shipments from the elevator to feed their chickens. By blocking truck traffic, the pickets were threatening Nova Scotia's poultry industry.

(Cops: left to right) Myself (black hat), Ron Mosher, Halifax Police Department (white helmet), and Sergeant Gordon McGrath, National Harbours Board (black hat) were the cops on duty during the Halifax Grain Elevator Strike (June 1, 1967).
Photographer unknown.

The fifth day of the strike, June 1, 1967, was the point of no return. If the farmers couldn't load their trucks and bring home feed, the chickens would die. Port officials, the Attorney General, and the farmers devised a plan. More than a dozen undercover plainclothes RCMP were mingling with the pickets and the onlookers, ready to arrest and remove any serious troublemakers. I had also stationed twenty harbour cops at the grain elevator to protect the grain truck unloading area. When the Port Police failed to convince the pickets to throw down their signs, 175 city police joined the crowd.

The strike broke when Halifax Police Chief Verdun Mitchell said something to the union president in a voice no one could hear. The union boss threw down his sign, shook his head, and walked off, leaving the other pickets in disarray. The strike fell apart soon after.

Brennan had overseen the entire operation, coordinated the various groups, and defused the threat. I felt more confident in him afterwards.

The first and second chiefs I had worked under used to tell me: "We can't do this," and "we'll have trouble with the Longshoremen's Union if we do that." Brennan was different. He was supportive. He'd say, "Good job, Billy", and "Make sure we cover this." He was always there in the background. It was the first time I was encouraged to do my job.

When I went home that night, Carol greeted me with a tall, cool rye and ginger, and one of my favourite meals: roast chicken!

Four months later I was keeping the cold storage plant under surveillance while trucks loaded frozen Thanksgiving turkeys and rumbled out of the yard, to all corners of the province. I spotted a familiar vehicle leaving the plant. When I noticed that the driver was a young boy—he couldn't have been more than sixteen—I signalled for him to pull over. I questioned him and his buddy and they tripped on their words. Their nervousness became even more obvious when I told the driver to open the trunk. Inside was an opened case of beer and four cases of frozen lobster meat packed twenty-four cans to a case.

"How do you account for the beer and the lobster?" I asked the driver.

"I'm doing a delivery for my father," he said, as if that put him above the law.

"Well, who in the hell is your father?"

"A shipping manager."

OK. Now, this is getting interesting...

"Where's the receipt?" I asked.

"Don't have one."

"Well, I'm placing you under arrest for transporting open liquor, and you're coming with me to the police station."

It didn't take long for the shipping manager and his lawyer, Leo Rooney, to arrive at the station. Brennan, who had previously been in charge of the cold storage plant, arrived soon afterwards. I had charged the boy with theft and possession of stolen goods and I was about to charge his father with theft when Leo took me aside. "Billy," he said in a half-whisper, "the shipping manager has thirty-two years of service. Charge him, and his job and pension are gone. I'll

give you a deal. Charge only the driver and he'll enter a plea of guilty to possession. Charge the head shipper and we'll fight you all the way."

If the driver were to plead not guilty, his father would have enough time to
write a receipt for the stolen goods and give it to him before the trial.

I needed time to consider my options so I poured myself a coffee and offered some to the others present, in much the same way that I used to kill time
by jumping out of the wrestling ring to a count of twenty before re-entering the
fight.

Brennan knew that the canned lobster belonged to the plant and as Police
Administrator, he'd have to back me up. But he and I both knew that charging
the head shipper would open a huge can of worms because everyone would
be squealing on everyone else to save their own ass: checkers, shippers, plant
workers, truckers, and even the cops who were paid to look the other way. I knew
that the accused would never be convicted in court with a receipt. I wouldn't be
getting what I wanted, but I figured it was better than nothing.

After sipping my coffee for two or three minutes I turned to Leo and said,
"Bring the kid to court tomorrow morning and enter a plea of guilty, and that
will be the end of it." And then I played my trump card: "Leo, try entering a plea
of not guilty and I will go through the cold storage plant like a dose of fucking
Ex-Lax, charging everyone from top to bottom with everything I can."

The boy pled guilty in court and was fined $300.

It was going to be hard to nail the people at the top, and this case proved it.
The kid took the fall, while the real crooks kept going.

To his credit, Brennan did not interfere with this case. He stood by at the station, supporting me in his own quiet way. He could have pressured me to tread
lightly, knowing how much shit I could disturb if I wanted to. But he just let me
do my job, and I respected him for that.

The Desk Sergeant tore a strip off me because I failed to notify him at the
time of the offence. He had never made an arrest in his life, and he had the gall
to give me a letter of reprimand!

The next direct contact I had with Brennan was when he called me to his office in June 1968. "Tomorrow," he said in a serious tone of voice, "have yourself
and the other sergeants at the admin building at two pm to meet your new
boss." Then he extended his arm and shook my hand, and said, "Thanks for
everything."

The other sergeants and I waited at the appointed time, nervous because we
were afraid of the unknown, and excited about the changes to come.

In a matter of minutes, in walked a six-foot tall Mountie. He had an unmistakable air of authority. Carrying himself as straight as a ramrod, his arms
swung at his sides as if he were marching. Right away I noticed his spotless
attire: starched white shirt, salt-and-pepper sports coat, and grey slacks—all
perfectly pressed—a distinguished-looking tie, the crease in his pants so sharp

it looked dangerous, and fiercely polished black shoes. Even though he was in civilian dress, he wouldn't have looked any more like a Mountie had he been dressed in a red coat and spurs. Expressionless, he said to me, "Sergeant, stand the men easy."

At that instant a smile broke across his face like a shaft of sunlight hitting the shade. "Good afternoon, gentlemen," he began. "My name is Alex ("Alec") Taylor and I am the new Superintendent of Police. You will be working directly under my supervision." He spoke very slowly, as if weighing every word. "You will be answering only to me."

Immediately, I felt relieved. We were accustomed to having to answer to every sonofabitch at the Port, which turned a lot of investigations to mush. I sensed that with Alex I would get the unconditional backing I needed—from the top, for the first time.

On that first day Alex only said a few words. He finished up by saying, "Gentlemen, I have come here to restore law and order to the waterfront. And make no mistake: law and order will be restored." Then he told me to dismiss the men (stand them easy). We made small talk with him for ten or fifteen minutes—telling him who we were, how long we had been there, and what we were up to. Little did we know that Alex probably knew more about us than we knew about ourselves! He had thoroughly investigated every member of the Port Police, Halifax Detachment through his contacts with the RCMP and Halifax City Detective Division.

Alex left me with the impression he would be fair—but don't ever cross him!

It was no fluke that our new Chief was committed to smashing the theft rings on the Halifax waterfront. The events that led to Alex's appointment began with a complaint that was laid by the Insurance Underwriters of Canada in 1966. The increase in waterfront theft had forced the insurance companies to jack up their premiums. The higher costs were threatening to choke off Canada's import/export trade. Under the authority of Prime Minister Lester B. Pearson, Parliament appointed Donald N. Cassidy to look into the problem. After a thorough investigation, the retired Criminal Investigator and RCMP Staff Sergeant Major came back to Parliament with fifty-seven recommendations. Parliament threw the ball right back into Cassidy's court, instructing him to implement all of his recommendations!

In 1968, the separate police forces that had been operating at Canadian ports under the National Harbours Board were reorganized into one national force, the Ports Canada Police.

Cassidy had spent two years in intelligence-gathering and planning, and that year he hired retired RCMP and city police officers to head every port in Canada. He picked Alex Taylor to be Superintendent at the Port of Halifax. Curbing waterfront theft had become the top priority, and that's when I was promoted to sergeant. At the time, I was the most senior member of Ports Canada Police in the country. So I received Badge #1.

Photograph by Lysia Taylor.

I didn't realize it that first day, but I had crossed paths with Alex many years earlier—in 1947 at an annual Woodsmen's Exhibition in Beaver Dam, Shelburne County. For the first two days woodsmen competed, standing on logs in a lake, rolling logs, climbing trees, and climbing poles. On the third day there was a professional wrestling match. It was a fixed tag-team match featuring Bill Rhyno from Liverpool, Curly Elguire from Halifax, Frank Hoskins (the "Hooded Secret") from Halifax, and myself. I vaguely recall seeing a Mountie observing the activities, and Alex recalls hearing me say: "Watch out for that goddamn Mountie!"

My claim was that any spectator who could stay in the ring with me for five minutes would win a five-dollar bill. Right away two six-foot lumberjacks who were drunker than me accepted the challenge and each one lasted about two minutes. I made sure to get them off their feet early in the game—my sure-fire way to beat tall wrestlers—and then my trusty step-over toe hold finished them off. The moonshine and bootlegged liquor was flowing freely that day. That's why Alex Taylor was there.

When he was a two-year-old toddler in 1927, Alex's family immigrated to Transcona, Manitoba from Belfast, Ireland. As a teenager he showed great promise as a hockey player in the Manitoba Hockey League. When I met with him nine years ago, he was seated in his Dartmouth, Nova Scotia home. The seventy-seven-year-old fondly recalled two businessmen in suits approaching him at the rink when he was seventeen.

"Mr. Taylor, we've been watching you the last couple of weeks, and we think you could make the Chicago Blackhawks," one of them said, full of confidence. He held up a contract and said they would pay $4,000 if Alex signed.

"Then they told me to talk to my father about it," Alex recalled. "Well, that was more than he made in a year! I found my dad in the crowd, told him about their offer, and came back with him.

"He looked at the men and said, 'The boy has got to get himself a job as a carpenter or an electrician. I don't know what this goddamn hockey is all about.'"

That was the end of Alex's hockey career.

After joining the RCMP in 1941, Alex was stationed in Edmonton, Calgary, Lethbridge, and Cardston, Alberta before transferring to Nova Scotia where he was named Chief Investigator in the Criminal Investigation Branch. After twenty-six years of service, in 1967 he ended his police career as Staff Sergeant of "H" Division at the Halifax Criminal Investigation Branch. He went on to set up the family court system in Halifax. That's when Cassidy asked Alex to head up the Ports Canada Police in Halifax.

"He didn't explain anything," Alex recalled with a half-smile.

When he told retired Halifax Police Department Sergeant Nels Goulding about the appointment, Nels said, "You're a goddamn idiot for going to the waterfront!"

Alex's partial smile broke into a grin. "You see, I didn't know what was going on there."

Alex Taylor and myself remembering
old times at Alex's home in Dartmouth, 2002.
Photograph by Andrew Safer.

He soon found out that at least one-third of the Port Police were involved in the theft rings—typically by accepting bribes and favours to look the other way.

At the first hint of winter the shipping season got underway and we set up roadway spot checks at Pier 9 (Richmond Terminal), Pier 2 (Deep Water Terminal), and Piers 20 to 40 (Ocean Terminals). The first week we found enough stolen clothing, shoes, radios, televisions, tools, and furniture to fill a thirty-foot rig. We put it all in a locked wire enclosure known as a shed crib. That was the first time Alex saw evidence of theft on the waterfront.

Soon after Alex took over as Chief, he discovered my drinking habit. On the day before Christmas in 1968, an RCMP Intelligence officer handed me a forty-ouncer of rye, wrapped in Christmas paper. This was to show his appreciation for some investigative work I had done in conjunction with the RCMP. Towards the end of my shift, at around eleven o'clock at night, I walked into the lunch-room with the forty-ouncer, half a dozen paper cups, and some club soda. Six constables were seated at the table. Alcohol wasn't allowed at the police station but that didn't concern me at the time. A special occasion called for special treatment. I poured a couple of rounds of drinks for the men. At eleven-thirty I handed the bottle to the shift sergeant who was coming on to relieve me.

"Here," I said. "Give the men a Christmas drink when they leave."

I had the next week or so off. On January second, my first day back, Alex called me into his office first thing.

It was around nine o'clock. He was seated at his desk when I strolled in. I wasn't quite back into the swing of things after a week of partying, but as soon as I saw the Chief I snapped to attention and saluted him. I knew there was something wrong because instead of his customary smile he looked stern. He didn't give me much time to speculate.

"Were you drinking on duty Christmas Eve?" Alex asked sharply, his eyebrows drawn together to a point. His steady eyes were fixed on mine.

"Yes, Sir," I said without hesitation.

"Did you have a bottle of liquor in your possession at the station on Christmas Eve?"

If he was asking about it, I figured he must know. Again I replied, "Yes, Sir."

"Were any of your men drinking on duty on Christmas Eve?" It was obvious he knew.

"Yes, Sir."

At that point, he opened his top left drawer, took out the bottle of rye, and stood it on his desk. The liquor level hadn't changed since I had passed it on to the next shift sergeant.

Alex continued his line of questioning. "Is this the bottle you had on Christmas Eve?"

"Yes, Sir."

By this time I was sweating gumdrops. There wasn't anything to prevent the Chief from firing me on the spot. I stood there in silence for ten to fifteen seconds, which seemed like hours. Finally Alex said, "It's a good thing you told me the truth. Had you lied to me I would have fired you. Needless to say, I'll never have to speak to you about alcohol again."

"I promise, Chief," I said, stressing each word with feeling. "You will never have to speak to me again about having a bottle of booze on duty. I promise." With that, he dismissed me.

For the rest of the day I thought about how much trouble booze can cause, and I finally concluded that the best solution was to not get caught. I figured out how to avoid bringing a bottle to work.

When I went to work the next morning I carried six oranges in a brown paper bag. The night before I had injected them with as much vodka as I could squeeze into them. I rationalized that I wouldn't be able to concentrate on my job otherwise, because I'd be too busy scheming how to get booze. This way, I was solving that problem in advance. Every night I grabbed my trusty hypodermic needle and filled a bunch of oranges, pears, and any other fruit that would hold booze so I never had to worry about keeping my word with Alex. I never brought another bottle in to work again as long as Alex was there, so help me God!

The days I didn't bring fruit to work I visited ships that were moored at the Port. By chewing whole cloves of garlic (a holdover from my wrestling days), I not only masked my breath, but also made sure that no one got too close. I looked squeaky clean because I never took a bottle of the crew members' liquor off the ships. Instead, I loaded up while on board and carried it ashore in my gut.

Looking back at that now, I see how proud I was for pulling the wool over the boss's eyes. But deep down, I felt guilty as hell. Here was Alex, doing everything he could for me, sending me—above everyone else—on the best police training courses. And what was I doing? Deceiving him by drinking behind his back! I managed to cover up my guilt by working my butt off (I became a workaholic). Another way I hid my shame was by overcompensating. I was extra kind and generous to my family and close friends. I kept deceiving myself and others for many years.

At about the time of the fruit-and-booze caper, I started thinking I could be a lot more effective if I was working with a partner. Denny was the only other cop in the detachment who thought the way I did about crooks. He'd go after anybody for anything, relentlessly and viciously, if that's what was called for. Ever since I made that snide remark about the raincoat the day we met, we had stayed out of each other's way. I surprised him when I showed up in his office one afternoon.

After making small talk, I started in: "Denny, you and I seem to be thinking and doing along the same lines with waterfront workers. Why don't we try to do this together instead of by ourselves?

Right away, he warmed up to the idea. "OK," he said, "let's give it a shot."

We also agreed that since we didn't like each other, we'd keep it to a strict business relationship. We just wanted to get the job done.

"After we're finished with work, I don't want to have anything to do with you," I said. "I don't want to talk to you until we come to work the next day."

"Yeah, I was thinking the same thing."

As it turned out, over the years we and our wives and kids wound up spending a lot of time together socializing, contrary to what we first thought.

It wasn't long before Denny and I were the loose cannons of the Port Police. We knew some of the movers and shakers in the organized theft rings—some of the senior police, port officials, gang bosses, shore captains (the men who hired the gangs for the shipping companies), and longshoremen—which meant we could hold valuable information over their heads. They knew we could expose their involvement if they tried to stop us, which put us in an unusual position of power.

Myself and Sergeant Ed Kirby. Stolen goods, seized in a house raid in Eastern Passage on February 14, 1969 included footwear, clothing, radios, china, and a guitar.
Courtesy Halifax Police Department.

When we did stakeouts—if one of us was in a cruiser and the other was on foot—we always arrived to close in on our target within a minute of each other. Neither of us ever backed away from a challenge, nor did we ever show up late.

One afternoon we were getting ready to nab a longshoreman who had stolen a pair of boots from Shed 23. This seemingly small-time theft was bigger than it looked. For some time, Bob had been a decoy to divert us from a sizable cargo theft operation. A week earlier we had apprehended him, made him take off his boots, and marched him out to the police car barefoot in the snow! But before we could charge him with theft, we had to prove ownership. It wasn't so easy because that meant we had to track down the consignee of the goods in transit at the time of the theft. We finally received proof of ownership. We had the boots, and now we were going back for the body that went with them.

It was five o'clock when we showed up at Pier 36. Bob was just coming off shift. Suddenly, about 100 longshoremen surrounded Denny and me. Bob was holding a hatchet. He and his buddies were in the section of Shed 36 that was usually reserved for cargo. The stevedores were shouting that they were going to throw us in the harbour. Denny and I broke through the crowd, disarmed and handcuffed Bob, put him in the police car, and drove off. It worked because the stevedores knew that if they had laid a hand on us we would have drawn our guns and fired if we felt our lives were in danger.

One evening in January 1969, I was at home when an informant phoned to say that clothing was being stolen from a Maersk ship docked at Pier 9. I called Denny's house and we drove down to Pier 9—me in my 1965 cream-topped green Buick Special, and Denny in an unmarked police cruiser. We parked at the head of the Pier 9 roadway and set up a vehicle spot check. A ten-foot-high wire fence on either side of the road made it difficult for motorists to approach and then turn around and head back. We knew the license plate numbers of the suspects' cars so we sat there in the dark with binoculars checking plates. At about seven-thirty a dark late-model Ford sedan whose license plate matched one of the sets of numbers approached well within the twenty mile-per-hour speed limit. We pulled out and parked in the middle of the highway. I turned on my portable roof flashers. We got out and flagged them down with flashlights.

The two men were in their forties. Denny asked them to step out of their car, which they did with no argument. We searched the car with our flashlights and there was nothing inside. The driver offered to open the trunk. We refused. We had information that they were wearing the stolen goods so we didn't want to waste any more time searching the car.

"Unbutton your coats," I instructed.

"What for? We don't have any liquor on us," one of them said in a smart-alecky voice.

When he heard this, Denny fired back: "You either start unbuttoning your coat or Taylor's going to start a wrestling match with you guys and he's going to unbutton your coats for you."

They were wearing old red-and-black checkered hunting jackets. When they unbuttoned the jackets there was nothing suspicious-looking underneath. The other one said, "See, there's no liquor under here."

"Now, take off your pants," I barked. They looked at each other as if they wanted to get back in the car and leave. Then they jeered at us, making lewd comments about why we would want them to take off their pants. That's when I said: "Take your pants down or we're going to shoot them off you." At that point, I think they knew that we knew.

They unbuttoned and unzipped their pants, and new brown dress slacks appeared underneath. The short one shot back: "I always wear two pairs of pants." We told them to keep on peeling them off. Sure enough, there was another pair underneath, and another one under those, until they said they had each removed a dozen pants! Finally, they stood there in the dark, buck naked, except for their drawers. The pants were heaped in a pile.

One at a time, we threw the pants on the hood of their car, and then transferred them to the trunk of the police cruiser. We drove them to the station where each signed a statement admitting to the theft of twelve pairs of pants. We arrested them, tying up and marking the pants as exhibits. Just when I thought this case was in the bag I counted my suspect's pants and there were only eleven! Like a dummy, I had relied on the sonofabitch to tell me how many pairs of pants he had been wearing. Now I had a statement claiming twelve pairs that wouldn't hold up in court!

This was an important case because it was one of the first since Denny and I began working together, and because it would set a precedent for prosecuting this common type of theft of goods in transit. I was also feeling competitive with Denny, not wanting him to get a conviction without me. I didn't want to risk losing the case. After midnight, Denny and I took a trip over to the shed where the stevedores had unloaded the pants from the ship, and I stole a pair. It was the only way to be sure my statement would stand up in court.

That night I didn't sleep a wink. I felt guilty for stealing the pants. Hell, I wasn't any better than the criminals. But there was a lot riding on this case. It could open the door to breaking the organized theft rings. On the other hand, we didn't have a clue as to what we were doing. Even the prosecutor was unsure how to proceed with a theft case involving goods in transit, and how to prove ownership. My mind was racing all night as I tried to see all the angles.

The next morning, after several coffees, I showed up for work groggy and confused. I went in to Alex's office to get some advice. I was about to tell him about the pants I'd swiped when he cut me off. "Excuse me," he said with authority. "I don't want to hear any more about it. It's your case. You handle it the way you think you should." I decided to go to court with the eleven pairs of pants (leaving the one I had swiped behind) and the statement, and hope for the best, rather than risk perjuring myself in court pretending this guy had stolen twelve pairs.

I told the prosecutor that the information should read eleven pairs of pants, not twelve, and he requested that the court amend it. A guardian angel must have been watching over me. Now we had the amended information going to trial!

A piece of information that came our way the day before the trial shed some light on the circumstances of the theft. We thought the pants had been stolen at Shed 9b but in fact, they had been lifted from the deck of the ship, as "over-stowed cargo"—cargo lashed to the ship's deck when the hold is filled to capacity. That meant that the ship was the owner of the goods. This was important because our original plan was for the shipping company to claim ownership in court. Instead, we had to track down the ship's chief officer. He agreed to testify.

If you ever want to get on the bad side of a ship's chief officer, just steal his cargo. On the witness stand, this gentleman in his neatly pressed uniform produced all the papers needed to claim ownership. He took the time to explain to the court about over-stowed cargo and other shipping terminology relevant to the case. It was a historic day because it was the first time a ship's manifest had ever been presented in Provincial Courtroom Number One to prove ownership.

It was our turn to give evidence. Judge Murray tore Denny and me to shreds for the way we had spoken to and handled the suspects, and he threw out our written statements. We looked like a couple of dumb Keystone cops.

At the end of the three-hour trial, Judge Murray ordered the two accused to stand before him. "I find you both guilty," he said solemnly, fining them $300 each, plus costs. Then he turned to the waterfront workers in the courtroom. "A word of advice to all present here today. Theft of commercial goods will not be tolerated in the port city of Halifax. This is not just a word of advice. It's a word of warning to the waterfront unions."

In spite of our shoddy performance, we got the conviction! I returned the pair of pants to its box in the shed, and headed back to the police station. It was six o'clock. I was surprised to see Alex's light on because he always went home at four o'clock sharp. I knocked on his door and went in. He was sitting at his desk, looking glum. This was a test case under Alex's new command. In a low voice, as if he were about to scold me, he said, "Well...What happened?" He was bracing for the worst.

"Sir, both were convicted," I said triumphantly. (As it turned out, both thieves were convicts who had served time in Dorchester Penitentiary.)

Alex's face lit up. He stretched his arms high above his head and cried, "Yes, yes, yes!"—like a child at Christmas.

I found out later that every port chief in Canada was tuned into this case. Even Director General Cassidy in Ottawa had asked Alex to call him at home with the results—a call Alex made later that evening.

This looked like a nickel-and-dime theft case over a few lousy pairs of pants, but because it set a precedent in Nova Scotia for proving ownership of goods in transit, it was a landmark case for the Port Police. I later found out that the transcript of the court proceedings had been sent to every port in Canada, and incorporated into a training course at the police training school in Ottawa.

On January 30, 1969 I received a letter of commendation from Chief Taylor for my part in the pants case. It was one of thirty letters of commendation I would receive during my police career—but I would receive more letters of reprimand for my unpredictable and unruly behaviour.

Partly because of my work on the pants case, Alex sent me to the RCMP "N" Division in Ottawa to take a two-week course in Criminal Investigation.

Participants in a Criminal Investigation course, RCMP
"N" Division, Ottawa, 1969. I'm seated in the front
row, third from the right. Photographer unknown.

The instructors were the top men in the Investigation field. One was a retired RCMP Inspector who had been an expert in the recruitment and development of informants. I can still see him today standing in front of the class in his white suit, yellow shirt and tie, two-tone Bermuda shoes, and a white straw dip hat.

After two gruelling weeks of studying twelve hours a day, including weekends, I was amazed to find out I had finished at the top of my class! Considering that most of the others had college degrees, I was feeling pretty good about myself the day we received our certificates. When I returned, I brought back some powerful tools I could use on the Halifax waterfront.

The more Alex did for me, the worse I felt about deceiving him with the booze. He had sent me on course, and now he was looking into more training for me. The worse I felt about it, the more I drank.

I drank to overcome my problems which were created by drinking.

Soon after I was back, Alex told Denny and me to start dressing in plain-clothes to boost our chances of infiltrating the theft rings. He gave us free rein when it came to dress code, hours, and stakeouts. Whereas Brennan had supported me in his own quiet way, Alex turned up the volume. He was convinced that Denny and I could help him clean up the waterfront. With his vote of confidence, I started doing the kind of work I had been wanting to do for years.

Denny and I dogged criminals night and day, sometimes busting in on them at four o'clock in the morning, grabbing a few hours' sleep, and then going back at it. Now that stevedores and checkers were fair game, work was getting a lot more interesting. The more arrests we made, the more it seemed we were only scratching the surface—the outer ring of a complex and well-oiled underground operation.

We realized that much of our police work wouldn't stand up to a "not guilty" plea in court. We had learned from the pants case that it all boiled down to proving ownership. When we caught someone red-handed stealing clothing, small appliances, fish, hardware, or anything else the buggers could carry off or load into a car, that wasn't enough to make a case. First we had to identify the legal owner at the time of the theft, and then we had to ensure that a representative of that organization would testify in court.

That wasn't so easy. Let's say a manufacturer in Hong Kong had contracted with a shipping line to transport a carton of shoes to Sears in Halifax through the Port of Halifax. The stevedores unload it at Shed 32, and it's stolen. Who was the legal owner at the time of the theft? Sears hadn't received the goods yet, so it wasn't them, and the manufacturer had released the goods to the shipping line so they were no longer the owner. In fact, the shipping company was the legal owner. The only problem was the shippers didn't want to present documentation in court because they were afraid of upsetting the stevedores who would then refuse to unload their ships.

The pants case had spoiled us into thinking that catching thieves was as easy as shooting fish in a barrel. Sure, we could catch them, but getting a conviction was another matter. Once we knew that the pants had been stolen on board ship, getting the ship's chief officer to testify in court was a no-brainer. But since most of the thefts took place in the sheds, identifying the owner was more difficult. The second hurdle was getting the owner to testify in court despite the possible consequences.

Our lawyers in Ottawa told us that "any person, organization, or company that has custody and control of such goods shall be deemed to be the lawful owner of such goods", as long as they have the proper documentation. We met with the shipping companies and asked each of them to designate a representative who could appear in court. After about six months of losing this cat and mouse game, we finally succeeded in getting shipping agents such as

I. H. Mathers to play ball. I was able to interest them in cooperating because I knew the boss's son, Harry. They weren't afraid to appear in court and produce the paperwork needed to convict the thieves because they didn't have a direct relationship with the stevedores.

This pushed the thieves to find out-of-province markets for the goods, which turned out to be mainly Saint John and Montreal. Many of the stolen items that were circulating in Halifax were being shipped in from Saint John and Montreal, and vice versa. Suddenly, it became extremely difficult for us to obtain the evidence we needed for convictions. As it turned out, our early successes in court motivated the crooks to develop an inter-provincial network. Catching them now would require much more sophisticated methods.

Sometimes, even with the proper documentation, we knew we wouldn't be able to obtain a conviction in court. In these cases, we charged the individuals under the Customs Act. We would then seize the goods—such as imported liquor—and charge them for not having paid the duty. (The person who was in possession of the goods had to prove that the duty had been paid.) The penalty was almost as stiff as the penalty for theft and possession.

7. ALL IN A DAY'S WORK

While some of the more sophisticated crooks were taking their trade out of province, others were devising deadly ways of intimidating and terrorizing the cops walking the beats at the piers.

Sometimes they would bait us. One time a girl ran up to a cop on Marginal Road. Her nose was bleeding and her blouse was ripped open. "He tried to rape me!" she cried, pointing to an alley. The cop ran into the alley and was beaten so badly he never worked again. Sometimes they would remove a manhole cover and then, at night, lure the cops into their trap.

We had an unmarked car keeping a constant patrol on the comings and goings at the Halterm container terminal during non-working hours, between 10:00 pm and 5:00 am. One night a group couldn't get in through the gate so they arranged to come in on a motorboat, alongside the pier. Their plan was to make off with the liquor from several containers they had left out during the day shift.

A spreader is a twenty-ton piece of equipment. Attached to a crane, it picks up the containers and moves them on and off the ships. At the end of each shift, for safety reasons, the longshoremen are supposed to raise the spreaders to the top of the cranes and leave them there. On this night, the workers left the spreaders down at the level where they would just clear the engine bonnet on a car. In the dark, there was a good chance the cop doing rounds wouldn't see it. The spreader would smash through the windshield, and everything else in its way.

That night, Wayne was driving an unmarked police car through Halterm, checking on containers. He must have just caught a glimpse of the spreader from the corner of his eye, when it was inches from his windshield. He ducked between the dashboard and the front seat just before it crashed through. Afterwards, he told us he looked up and saw it swinging over the car a few times before settling in one spot above him in mid-air. The car was still running so he radioed the other men on duty. Two beat cops and two cops in unmarked cars rushed to the scene within minutes, and fished him out. Aside from minor scrapes, Wayne was fine—he didn't even have to go to the hospital. It was a miracle he was alive. If he had reacted a moment later, the spreader might have decapitated him.

Police car mobile #3 after colliding with the spreader, head-on.
Photograph by Billy Taylor.

After beating our brains out trying to deal with stolen goods in transit—in the sheds, on board ships, and elsewhere on port property—I was given a different kind of case. It involved the theft of dollar bills.

In the fall of 1970, Alex received a call to investigate a theft that had taken place on board a bulk cargo ship between the time it was loaded in Venezuela and the time it docked at Pier 2 South. He called me into his office.

"Billy, I want you and Denny to investigate a theft," he instructed. "One thousand two hundred and eighty dollars has gone missing from the Captain's cabin on board a cargo vessel that's come in from Aruba. The Captain swears his cabin was locked when the theft occurred, and he says it happened since the ship docked in Halifax."

"How long ago did this happen, Sir?" I asked, wondering how in the hell we were going to get a toehold in this case.

"Three days ago. Whoever took it, it's probably mostly spent by now. And the ship is leaving tomorrow so there's not a whole lot we can do, but let's give it our best shot." He knew it would be impossible to interrogate all 100 stevedores and 35 crew—all of whom would be suspects in this type of case. He didn't even have any paperwork to give me. I went back to my desk, thinking that Alex had probably given us this case because we were the only cops who dared to interrogate longshoremen. Denny and I arranged to meet at the ship in half an hour.

I figured the Captain was pulling a fast one—taking his own money and then hoping to double it through an insurance scam. When we arrived at the ship and spoke to him, that didn't appear to be the case.

Questioning the crew we learned that one member had recently purchased a couple of record albums and some articles of clothing. Figuring that a six-foot-tall black man who spoke broken English wouldn't be too hard to find in downtown Halifax, we went to the most popular tavern among waterfront workers, the Peppermint Lounge in the Trade Mart Building. Finding no one there matching the description, we returned to the ship and waited. He appeared around midnight, identifying himself as Cam Hayden from Aruba. Even in our plainclothes, we must have been convincing because he allowed us to take him to the spare office in Shed 2. We closed the doors, showed our badges, and said we wished to speak to him about an urgent matter.

Figuring the money was on him, we stripped him down to his skin and searched him, but only found about four dollars in Canadian change. With each passing moment he was getting more and more nervous. I told Denny I wanted to continue the questioning, and he left me alone with Hayden for two or three minutes.

"Listen to me you sonofabitch," I said to him as if I was shooting. "If you don't give me the money you stole you're going to spend the rest of your fucking life in a Canadian prison."

When Denny came back, Hayden was telling me where he had stashed the dollar bills in his cabin. Back at the ship, the three of us squeezed into his tidy five- by eight-foot quarters which contained a bed, a table, and a lamp. Hayden walked over to the head of the bed, leaned forward, and, popping off the ceiling moulding, he exposed a one-eighth-inch space between the ceiling and the compressed cardboard wall. Looking over at me to make sure I was watching, he snapped open a steel pocket knife and inserted its point in the crack. Motioning with his free hand he showed me that this is where he had fed the dollar bills, one at a time. Removing a piece of wallboard was the next step.

"You wait here, Hayden," I said. "I'll go get a screwdriver and a hammer." When I handed him the tools, he popped off a few nails and exposed the insulation. It was littered with greenbacks, most of which had settled in a disorderly pile on the floor. In a matter of minutes he pulled out $1,150 from the wall cavity—only $130 shy of the amount stolen. We marched into the Captain's quarters and I handed him the bills. He stared in disbelief.

Hayden then explained his MO. Once the ship had docked, he cleaned the Captain's cabin, leaving a screw on the porthole window unfastened before locking the door on his way out. Later that night, he came back, pushed in the porthole, climbed in, took the money out of the Captain's drawer, and then locked the porthole from the inside. He locked the doorknob from the inside, and slammed the door behind him.

Hayden was deported to Aruba with a criminal record. Since the Captain wouldn't allow him back on the ship, the ship's agent paid for the plane ticket to fly him home. He was to pay the Captain the missing $130 from his future earnings. I wondered if that meant pulling another inside job on his next employer.

The Halifax Port Police, 1970. Alex Taylor: front row, fifth from left; Donald Cassidy: sixth from left; I'm the eighth from the left. Photographer unknown.

In the days before the containerization of cargo, all goods landed at the Port were either stacked in the transit sheds or, in the case of perishable food, in the Port's cold storage plant. From there, they were picked up by truck or rail. On a frosty February night I pulled my police cruiser into the lot in front of Shed 20 for a routine inspection. I opened the padlock on the north track-side door of Shed 20 and called out to the cargo watchman as I stepped inside.

Assigned to one of these rat-infested sheds for a twelve-hour shift, the watchman was to keep an eye on the goods stored there. Usually the general cargo was stacked thirty feet high—all the way to the angle-iron rafters. It was a huge space, stretching back 600 feet. The sheds were not heated, and the watchman was not allowed to park his car inside to supply his own heat. He wasn't even permitted to plug in a space heater.

On a quiet night, the cop on patrol would let the watchman into a small heated office at the shed's north end which was rented out to shipping companies during the day. That gave him a chance to relax, have some dinner, and stretch out for a snooze.

After business hours, only the cops had keys to the transit sheds.

As I walked up to Larry, the Shed 20 cargo watchman, I could tell he had something on his mind. A war veteran who was not well educated, he stood just five feet tall. About ten years older than me, he wore a heavy plaid jacket with a crumpled vest underneath, dark wool pants, and black work boots. Ruddy and dark, he had a scar on his right jaw. I'd spoken with him casually many times—enough to know that he never looked me in the eye. He seemed agitated as he stared at a spot on the floor.

"I hear you're fixing to crack down on the theft rings," he began tentative-ly. "Well, before you start looking at cargo watchmen, truckers, checkers, and longshoremen, maybe you'd better take a good look at yourselves."

"You must know something I don't," I said bluntly.

Larry was staring at the floor, unwilling to go further.

"Making insinuations isn't going to help me any," I offered after an uneasy silence. "If you have something to say, and names to name, there are a number of ways you can tell me. You can call me on the phone or you can leave a note somewhere—but if you leave a note, be sure to print it. Handwriting is easier to trace."

Larry still wasn't budging. I knew what was worrying him. Cargo watchmen were in the Cargo and Gangway Watchman's Union, which is affiliated with the Longshoremen's Union. If he spilled the beans on someone and I squealed, he could kiss his ass good-bye.

"Working in the sheds, it wouldn't be hard for a pile of cargo to fall on me, or for a machine to run me over."

"I can never squeal on an informant because if I did, that would be my last informant. No one else would trust me. I'd go to jail for contempt of court be-fore I'd reveal you as my source."

We carried on like this for a while and he finally felt comfortable enough to talk. The night before, he had been lying down on some cargo when he heard a rustling noise above the usual creaking of the shed's walls. Larry got up and walked down the track side of the 600-foot building, peering down the dimly lit pathways and the towering stacks of boxes. Although he hadn't seen anyone, he noticed that in one section the crates were arranged in a different order than before. These crates were filled with hats and shoes that were being shipped to Sears.

He suspected both the sergeant and the rookie cop who were on duty that night, since they had the only keys to the shed. Then he told me their MO for stealing cargo. While the cargo watchman was asleep in the office, they would rob the shed. I wondered if the prohibition against cars and space heaters was part of the cops' plan to force the watchmen to seek heat behind the office door.

By the end of the evening, I was armed with enough information to launch an investigation.

Down at the Port Police station, I told Inspector Charlie I had good information about two of our members, and explained what had happened at Shed 20. The Inspector just sat there with his hands in his lap, looking despondent. After a weighty pause, he leaned over, pressed the button on the intercom, and asked the Chief to come in. Charlie briefed the Chief as to what was going on.

"It really doesn't surprise me," the Chief said, "but that's the last thing I wanted to hear today." Turning to us, he said, "Sergeant Taylor and Inspector, you know what to do."

Charlie asked the Chief if he wanted to see the two suspects. The Chief just shook his head slowly from side to side.

The Inspector asked who the informant was, and I just smiled back.

"How much is this going to cost us?" he asked. I told him it wouldn't cost a cent. I explained if I played my cards right, this person would continue to give us good information for many years.

Only the Chief, the Inspector, and I knew the plan.

The sergeant and constable were on duty the next night. We figured they'd hit Shed 20 again, since they already had the list of contents in those boxes. We planted a cop in the shed, out of sight. Sure enough, well after dark, he saw two people rummaging through cargo. The light was so poor, he only saw two dark uniforms. When the two suspects went off duty at seven o'clock the next morning, we drew up a search warrant to search the sergeant's home. We also drafted letters of resignation for the two cops.

We stationed two marked police cruisers a few doors from the sergeant's home on the outskirts of Halifax. All they knew was that the cop would be bringing something from his house to the police station—and nowhere else. We had to keep everything else a secret from the entire force so no one could tip them off before we could catch them.

We brought the sergeant in for questioning and showed him the search warrant that specifically mentioned hats, shoes, and other articles of clothing—the contents of the boxes that had been tampered with in the shed. Once he saw the detail on that warrant, he knew we had him. He glumly volunteered to drive home, gather the goods, and bring them in.

If he were to call home and ask his wife to remove the items, the officers in the two marked cars would spot her. The Inspector drove an unmarked car to the sergeant's street and found a vantage point where he could see both the front door and the two cops stationed nearby. If he saw anyone leave the house carrying a box he'd radio the constables and tell them what to do. Instead, the sergeant showed up, lugged several boxes from his house, put them in his car, and drove off.

Four o'clock that afternoon at the police station, the Inspector gave the two crooks a choice. They could either sign their letters of resignation, or be charged with theft and possession of stolen goods under the Criminal Code.

As we expected, they resigned. The Inspector had me remove their firearms, and he ordered them to put their badges and IDs on his desk. Then they were dismissed.

The last thing the Port Police wanted was publicity that would implicate cops in the organized theft rings.

The plan went off without a hitch, but no one was celebrating. In fact, by eight o'clock that night, with the exception of Denny, the cops on the force weren't talking to me.

That wasn't the last time I ended up nailing cops. Some months later I was sent to Cornwall, Ontario for a supervisor's course. Other than top management, I was the only one who knew this course was also a sting operation involving one of our own top members. Management knew I was capable of such a task so they asked me to go.

The suspect, Sergeant Detective George Riley, was well respected throughout Ports Canada for his outstanding work arresting criminals and recovering stolen goods. He was a no-nonsense cop's cop.

After two days, I said offhandedly to George, "My wife had made plans for us and she was really pissed off that I had to go on course. When I go home I'm going to have to make it up to her somehow."

"Why don't you buy her a nice ring or a bracelet or something?" he asked.

"She's not much for jewellery," I said. "She's more of a clothes person, but I find it hard to buy clothes she likes."

That's when he came around to mentioning that his family was in the jewellery business. "I could get you a lovely ring or bracelet at cost," he said, looking at me convincingly. "I could sell you a bracelet for $500 that would easily be worth $1,500 to $2,000."

I didn't want my eagerness to tip him off so I said, "I don't know. I have to think about it. I'll mention it to Carol when I talk to her."

Towards the end of the week, George asked if I had brought it up with Carol.

"I told her I'm going to bring her back a nice gift, but didn't mention what it would be." I added I was still thinking about it.

During the second week I told him I liked the idea, and asked if he had any jewellery with him. He nodded, came back with a briefcase, and showed me a couple of rings and a bracelet. The bracelet caught my eye right away. It was gold, and it was inlaid with some fancy-looking stones. About three-quarters of an inch wide, it had an elegant design. It stretched through the fingers and onto the wrist, with no clasp.

I examined the bracelet and the rings closely. They looked like the real thing. I said I was impressed and I'd have to think it over. In the middle of the week I said I'd take the bracelet, and pay with a cheque. As I had figured, he wouldn't take a cheque so I told him I'd go to the bank and get the $500 in cash. On

Thursday, I gave him the $500, in marked bills, supplied to me by an under-cover cop, and he gave me the bracelet.

I had waited until the night before the end of the course so he wouldn't have much time to spend the money.

When he stepped off the plane at his home port, George was placed under arrest by the RCMP. They searched him and found the marked bills. They gave him the choice of either being charged with selling stolen goods, or signing his resignation. He resigned. Meanwhile, I had the evidence (the bracelet). I kept it until the case was closed, and then turned it in to the Ports Police office in Ottawa. If they needed further proof, they could have traced the bracelet back to the shipment which had come up short on the manifest.

A sergeant, George had worked for a long time in the Investigation branch, focusing mainly on theft! Informants had been telling us bits and pieces of what he was up to, so the top cops at the Port finally devised this sting operation to get to the bottom of it.

He and his longshoremen buddies had been lifting jewellery from cargoes as they arrived at the Port. Since he was one of the investigators, they had little to worry about. He had been making the odd recovery to show he was doing his job, while keeping most of it.

I had no problem nailing this guy. Greed had caused him to breach the trust the public had placed in him. To me, this is one of the worst offenses in any profession. Still, it wasn't pleasant nabbing one of our own guys.

It may seem like I wanted to nail every cop I could, but there was only one kind of cop I was interested in going after—the ones who abused the public's trust, like the cops in the cargo shed, and George.

8. HIT MEN AND SHRINKS DOGGING ME

My association with organized crime members involved with prostitution, gambling, loansharking, and bootlegging dates back to the early 1950s when I went to Montreal to wrestle in my late teens.

The least known of these four enterprises, bootlegging, was a multi-million dollar business operating in every Canadian port city. This wasn't just stealing a few bottles of booze and hiding them in an overcoat. The bootleggers were selling cargoes of liquor to Nova Scotian bars, clubs, and legions. In the days before containerization I saw sheds filled with 50,000 to 75,000 cases of liquor. Booze was much easier to steal back then, and it was harder to track.

Bartenders would buy stolen cases of liquor, hide them, and slip them into the bar's inventory when they got rid of a case of empties. That way, if the Nova Scotia liquor inspector paid a visit, they could account for the number of cases that had been purchased. At a dollar fifty a shot, they would take in fifty dollars for each bottle of rum, or six hundred dollars per case. After deducting what they had paid plus kickbacks to the inspector, cops, and their source inside the shipping company, they made a handsome profit.

I was never able to catch them in action. The closest I came was to intercept and seize a shipment that was being delivered to a Dartmouth club. After being charged with theft and possession, the driver was fined $1,000—pin money for the volume of business he must have been doing.

As for my early introduction to organized crime members in Montreal, a lot of the wrestlers went to a popular nightclub after the match, and I used to tag along. A well-known French Canadian wrestler owned and operated the club. This is where I first came into contact with gangsters. In their well-tailored suits, they came across as businessmen and gentlemen. I didn't get close with them, but we'd drink together.

The one I spent the most time with was a part-time wrestler who was 6' 4" and an impressive 280 pounds. He called himself Manuel Cortez and pretended to be Mexican, but he was really Italian. He had dark skin and jet black hair, and radiated confidence. Manuel always wore his signature three-piece black suit, a yellow necktie with a black shirt, and a black felt hat with a wide brim. He smoked the longest cigars I had ever seen. Always soft spoken, he acted like a gentleman. I had heard that he was a well-known Mafia godfather from Boston.

Fifteen years later, I was sitting on a bench in the dressing room at the Halifax Forum a few minutes before nine o'clock, waiting to referee a match. Two men approached me. Dressed immaculately, they were either big shots or a couple of gentlemen; it was hard to tell. Their finely tailored dark suits, white shirts, highly polished shoes, and expensive spectacles contrasted with the sweat and grime of the wrestlers.

"Billy, I've heard a lot of good things about your work with the organization," said one of them admiringly. "I've heard you're a policeman. We're sure proud of you. Listen," he stepped a little closer. "Any time you care to work for us—that's anywhere in the world where there's wrestling—just call our office in Houston."

"Well, thank you," I said offhandedly.

I didn't know what the hell he was talking about. It wasn't unusual for businessmen, doctors, and politicians to come into the dressing room to meet the wrestlers, so I wasn't too surprised. After they left, and just before the match, one of the wrestlers clued me in: "They're from the head office in Houston," he said. "They're nice guys—but don't ever cross them."

Then it hit me. Those guys were representing the North American Wrestling Alliance. They'd send someone up once a year to check the books to make sure the head office was getting its share of the gate receipts. Five per cent of my pay went to Houston and in return, I was guaranteed that no other referee would cut in on my territory. I was paying for "protection". No matter how gentlemanly these guys looked, I knew they could snap their fingers and find someone to do their dirty work on a moment's notice. In my half-cut condition, I forgot about them as soon as they left the room. The next day an RCMP officer approached me at work.

"I see your friends were here from the US," he said out of the blue.

"What do you mean?" I asked blankly.

"Those two businessmen. We followed them from the time they got off the plane to the time they boarded their flight home. We have nothing on them but we know what they do and who and what they're involved with."

He was talking about the locker room gents, but I didn't know why. And in my alcoholic state, I didn't much care. 'Well, that's your business,' I said to myself, before replying, "They're a couple of nice guys. They sure treated me decently, and that's all I know about them."

The next morning on the way to work I was rehearsing what I wanted to tell Alex. My shift members and I would be keeping a close eye on two known thieves we expected would be working the day shift on the waterfront. I reported to the Chief's office at eight o'clock for a routine briefing.

Docked from Piers 9 to 36, twelve ships from India, the British Isles, France, and Germany were filled with clocks, watches, clothing, household appliances, plywood, rubber, and auto parts. The thieves would be working as freight handlers, loading goods from Shed 23 into boxcars bound for eastern Canada and the US eastern seaboard.

I was thinking about these guys on my way to Alex's office. One had spent several years in the slammer for stabbing another hoodlum in Kentville. Shortly after his release he was caught in a bungled break and enter at Murphy's, a clothing store on Joseph Howe Avenue in Halifax. Along with his partner, they were the kingpins of the organized theft rings at the Port. Just about everything went through them.

All this was swimming through my head as I stepped into Alex's office. I saluted him and he waved me to be seated. After our customary chit chat, Alex casually took charge of the conversation.

"Billy," Alex said, "it has come to my attention that you have been associating with underworld crime figures connected with the professional boxing and wrestling business." He looked at me intently.

I was shocked.

In three years, Alex had never spoken to me about this. After a brief pause, he went on, in the offhand manner he had used so successfully as a top interrogator.

"It's not advisable for you to be associated with known crime figures, and be a policeman at the same time...particularly in the job you're doing. You have to make up your mind to be either a policeman or a wrestler."

'Are you insinuating that I'm playing both ends against the middle?' was my first reaction, which I thought but didn't say. I had been careful to never share police information with the people in the wrestling business, and vice versa. If I had told the wrestlers about police work, they would have figured that I'd just as easily squeal on them to the cops—and the same was true the other way around. No, I was a one-way mirror—and proud of it.

Alex was implying he didn't trust me. Maybe he even thought I was taking payoffs! 'Chief Taylor, you'd better take this job and shove it up your ass' is what I wanted to say. Instead, I sat there bolt upright—agitated, frozen, and tense.

Finally, I calmed myself and said, "This is what I do in my off-duty hours, on my own time. This is how I relax. There's no difference between wrestling and what the other sergeants do—fishing, hunting, and bowling, and it's the same as what you do, Sir. You coach hockey."

"But there *is* a difference," Alex insisted, still cordial. "You're being paid for what you do. It's not a hobby; it's a profession."

"Sir," I said, making up a story to protect myself, "the pay only covers my expenses: meals, drycleaning, and travelling." It was true that my expenses were higher than those of the other wrestlers because I usually travelled in my own car, with Carol, rather than ride with them in cars paid for by the promoter. What wasn't true was that there was nothing left after expenses.

Alex didn't answer for awhile. Finally, he said, "Our main concern (I noted his use of the word "our") is that you're going to get hurt in one of these matches and you won't be able to show up for work and perform your duty. If this ever happens, that will be the end of your time here. We'd have to ask for your resignation."

I knew I had him. "Cops who go fishing can drown; cops who go hunting can get shot," I said confidently. "I've seen you limp in here after a hockey game. There's less chance of me being hurt in a wrestling match than there is from crossing the street. Most people know that wrestling is fake, so how in the hell am I going to get hurt?"

"You have a point there. But I think you'd better give this very serious consideration."

I knew this was not a light matter that would just blow over. It doesn't look good for cops to be friends with gangsters. Realizing this could come down to a board hearing. I started planning my strategy with the same attention to detail I gave my cases.

'Always hold your cards close to your chest, Billy. Know when to play your trump cards and know when to fold.' "Lucky" Hanlan, a big-time professional gambler, had told me that and I never forgot it. I had met Lucky while working as a roustabout for the Bill Lynch Circus, after I quit school.

I opened my daily journal and, without naming names, made some notes about some of the people who used to go to the Bohemian Club, the wrestlers' favourite hang out in Montreal. One person who stood out in my mind was the wife of a famous NHL hockey player. She used to fraternize with the wrestlers while her husband was travelling with the team.

I was building a case to show that mainstream professional athletes were also associated with gangsters, either directly or by marriage.

Refereeing was just too profitable to give up. At the time, I was reffing four nights a week and doing a TV show on Wednesday mornings at CJCH. This went on for twenty-six weeks out of the year. My pay was between $800 and $1,000 a week, on top of which I was making $700 a week from police work. Carol was bringing in $500 a week as a bookkeeper for the federal government, so our combined income was quite high. (One-third of my pay, over $500 a week, went into booze, including partying, buying rounds, and leaving big tips.)

I thought about how poor we were when I was growing up—not having the right clothes, and bill collectors showing up at the door. There was no way I'd go back to that, and I was going to make damned sure my children didn't have to go through that either.

The next day I went to see my doctor and buddy, Kempton Hayes. I walked into his office looking distraught, and he cleared his schedule long enough to hear me out. I told him what had happened, that I was terribly upset, and that I felt discriminated against.

"If I have to quit my thing, everyone else should have to quit what they do too," I complained.

"Have you ever told these guys about the Police Department?"

"No. Never."

"Then they haven't got anything on you." Kemp added that he knew I wasn't the type of person to play both ends against the middle. He said he'd go to bat for me.

The next day, on my day off, I went in to see Alex. He greeted me in his usual friendly manner, and said, "I talked it over with Ottawa and they have no objections to your reffing on TV. But they don't want you to be involved in the wrestling business outside of TV because that's when you can come into contact with crime figures. Besides, as I said, if you get hurt and you miss work, that's it."

I decided to play my trump card. I was taking my chances, but I made it clear to the Chief that I would lay a complaint for discrimination if they made me stop refereeing outside of TV. Even though I had been hurt a couple of times wrestling, I had always managed to report for work.

Alex didn't give away what he was thinking, but I could hear the wheels turning. He was seriously considering what I'd just said.

In all fairness to Alex, one of his primary duties as Chief of Police was to make sure that all of the members could carry out their duties. He was just doing his job. He would have supported me in both professions had he been convinced of my ability to keep them separate.

At that time I was going to night school to upgrade my education. Shortly after I received my Grade Ten certificate from Sir John A. Macdonald High School on May 17, 1972, a group of psychologists and counsellors from Human Relations and Counselling came into the office to administer a questionnaire. These questions bothered me:

- Do you believe in God?
- Do you love your father?

• Do you love your mother?

These were not simple Yes/No questions. I suppose I believe in God, but I have my doubts, I thought. He never answered my prayers to make me taller. As for my father, there were a lot of things that went unsaid before he died in 1965.

At that moment I remembered a building where Dad took me when I was four years old. There were iron bars on the huge front doors. Dad spoke in a very low voice to a man in a uniform (a guard) and then we left a few minutes later. He looked very sad.

When I was in my thirties I paid a visit to Dorchester Penitentiary with Constable Vince Burque of the Halifax Police Department. As soon as I saw the prison I knew that this was the place where Dad had taken me as a small child some thirty years earlier. 'Why did we not see anyone other than the man in uniform?' I asked myself. 'Why was Dad so sad after he talked to the guard?'

'Why was it that Dad's youngest brother, Charlie, who worked as a long-shoreman on the Halifax waterfront all his life, never talked to me?'

'When Granddad Richard died he was buried in an unmarked grave. Who buried him and what happened to all his money?'

The answers to these questions are with my dad, his mother Susan, and his brothers and sister, who are lying next to each other in Halifax's Fairview Cemetery.

These are the questions that came to mind as I read the questionnaire.

It was painful stuff to have shoved right in my face at work. I answered 'Yes' to all three questions so they wouldn't have anything on me, and passed in the papers. I didn't hear from them for five months.

One rainy morning in the winter of 1972, Inspector Charlie and Chief Taylor called Denny and me into the Inspector's office. Second in command after Alex, Charlie was in charge of Operations. He stood over six feet tall, had an enviable build, and, with his Clarke Gable moustache, was good looking. Both Charlie and Alex were in their late forties at the time. The Inspector's office was even larger than Alex's office. What caught my eye as I walked in was the plush red carpet and the window looking out onto the track side of Shed 20.

As soon as we were seated, the Inspector locked eyes with me, and launched in: "From information we have received, there's a $10,000 hit contract out on you, and another on Denny, for the curtailment of the theft of cargo on the waterfront."

I could feel a smile creep across my face. "Well. That makes me feel like a celebrity!" I exclaimed. "I didn't know I was worth that much money, for some-body to do me in. I don't have that much life insurance on myself." I figured the tip had probably come through an undercover cop—RCMP Intelligence or a police informant.

Denny just sat there.

"Don't take this lightly," the Inspector continued. "Give it some thought." After a long pause, he looked at us and added, "Do you want bodyguards?"

I assumed he meant Halifax Police Department or RCMP. "No," I said. "I'm quite capable of handling myself in any situation that might come up."

"I don't care for any extra protection either," Denny said. "But if anybody bothers my family, they'll need more than a bodyguard!"

We told the Inspector we would just let this thing ride. Finally, the Chief said, "We cannot ignore this information. Be extra cautious."

Outside, Denny told me, "If anyone bothers my family, I'll kill the sonsabitches."

We told our wives and children to be extra careful who they talk to and where they go, and to not get into any strange cars. We were confident that no one would bother our families because it was common knowledge that if a criminal were to mess with a policeman's family, all hell would break loose.

I was mainly concerned with where my next drink was coming from. If it meant getting a drink, I would have gone into a den of thieves knowing that someone there wanted to kill me, so this threat went right over my head.

Ten thousand dollars a hit (twenty thousand dollars in total) was not all that much money when you think about the value of all the cargo that was being stolen from the docks. One shipment of footwear worth $10,000 had been stolen from a ship's cargo at Pier 39 and carted off in a trailer truck in a matter of minutes. That was just one of hundreds of heists that had been pulled off right under our noses each year.

It looked like someone was trying to get off cheap—getting rid of me and Denny for only ten bills apiece.

I only knew of one incident in the history of Halifax when a cop had been murdered. On July 14, 1924 a man by the name of Lewis Marshall Bevis was caught stealing household goods from a cottage on the Northwest Arm. He fled to Camp Hill Cemetery where, in a shoot-out with Halifax Police, he killed twenty-eight-year-old Constable Charles R. Fulton. On February 11, 1925 at 12:15 pm, Bevis became the second to last person to serve out the sentence of death by hanging in Halifax.

Cop killing was such a rare occurrence, I wasn't too worried.

The following evening I was on duty when the phone rang shortly after one o'clock. It was a young woman with a very pleasant, sexy voice.

"Billy, I have a lot of information for you about theft on the waterfront," she said.

"When and where can we meet?"

"I want to meet with you right now," she said. "Meet me at 1253 Barrington Street, Room Three."

It was not unusual to get calls from female informants. I wanted to talk to her as soon as possible.

I was familiar with this rooming house. An average-sized hotel, it was next door to Goldberg's Men's Wear on the south end of Barrington Street.

"While we're talking," she added, "I have a drink of rye for you, and anything else you'd like."

That told me it was a set-up. Informants want protection, revenge, and money; they don't do cops any favours. I ended the conversation with: "Yeah, I'll be right up"—but I never went.

Had I gone for the bait, she probably would have given me a few drinks and cozied up to me. Then some guys would bust in, rough her up a bit, maybe give her a black eye, say I was raping her, and shove a knife through me. She would have ended up with a chunk of the $10,000 hit money, and the thieves would be breathing easy.

Besides that call, the only indications I had that people were out to get me were the odd comment, like: "These two guys are going to go for a swim some day," and "The only good cop is a dead cop."

One Wednesday when I was plowing through paperwork, one of the desk sergeants came into the office to announce that all of the officers were going to Human Relations and Counselling to be interviewed. Eight of us reported to their office in Fenwick Towers where there were four interviewers.

As I walked into the cramped office, I noticed the carefully stacked papers on the desk. The windowless room with the dark brown, dingy carpet was depressing. A man of my height who must have weighed 250 pounds came forward to greet me. I recognized this fellow with thick-rimmed black glasses and dark, thinning hair. It was Marvin Burke. I knew him as a guitar player. I believed that all guitar players were drug addicts, so I took an immediate dislike to him. Besides, what qualified him to be talking to me? I sure as hell didn't come here to talk about music!

"The purpose of this interview," Marvin said as he sat squarely in his seat, "is to determine whether you are stable enough to carry a firearm." He proceeded to ask me a lot of personal questions, none of which were any of his goddamn business. I was, of course, half-cut at the time. He asked about my marriage, my children, and my home life when I was growing up—and I didn't like it one bit.

"Do you ever have any bad dreams?" he asked.

"Well, yes," I began, figuring this one I could answer. "One time I dreamt that I was on Clinton Avenue at my father's home. World War Two had ended, and the Japanese were invading Halifax. I was trying to protect my daughter; I was making sure the Japanese couldn't get hold of her. Somehow they had gotten into the house and they were creeping around with bayonets. I said to myself, 'No Japanese soldier is going to put a bayonet in my daughter,' and I choked her to death. I had this dream just after my daughter was born ten years ago, and it has bothered me ever since."

That's when Marvin ended the interview. I walked out of his office feeling that I had told the truth, so I was confident I would do OK on the test. Ten days later, Alex called me into his office. He was upset. His usual soft tone of voice was gone, his face stern.

"Billy, you've failed the psychological test," he said. "That means you can't carry a firearm."

I was dumbfounded.

Hell. How could I be a cop if I couldn't carry a gun? I was out of a job!

Myself at the Bedford Pistol Range, 1969.
Photographer unknown.

The Chief continued: "We've decided to have you re-interviewed by the head of the company—a Mr. Backman."

I'll pass this thing with flying colours, I thought. This time I just won't say anything about my dreams.

When I walked into Ron Backman's office the next week, I saw what a difference it makes to own the company! His quarters were twice as big as Marvin's. The carpet was thicker and the room was much brighter because there were two large windows looking out onto the city.

The well-groomed Backman wore a dark business suit. He spoke in a casual and friendly voice about the testing, and then asked if it was OK to record our conversation. I said No, and he proceeded to ask the same questions as before except he didn't ask about dreams. After a couple of minutes, I figured I was getting the shaft. How could he pass me after one of his employees had already failed me? I sat back in my chair and said to myself, 'This is not going to work.'

Backman was still questioning me when I stood up and announced, "I have nothing more to say. I think you've heard it all. Good day." I walked out.

The next week I was checking cargo in the area between Pier 23 and Pier 25 when the dispatcher called for me on my portable radio. I was to report to the Chief's office right away.

Standing at attention, I looked the Chief in the eye. He was dead serious. I figured it must be about the test. "Sergeant, may I have your revolver?" he said in a businesslike voice. "Take it out and unload it please."

I took out my revolver and opened the cylinder, pushed the ejection rod to remove the shells, and passed it over to him. Then he told me I'd failed the psychological test.

I felt empty inside.

"If you care to resign from the department," the Chief said, "we will guarantee you a lifetime job as a civilian employee with the force." He was seated. I remained at attention.

"This guarantee of a lifetime job would only be good as long as you are here," I said as calmly as I could, to mask my anger. "The minute a new chief takes over, that guarantee wouldn't mean dick to him."

"You're probably right."

My police career is over, I thought. And what other job can I get since everyone is going to think I'm a psycho case?

I saluted the Chief and left his office—without my gun. Over the next two days I went through two forty-ouncers of rye. Later that week I was desperate to talk to someone, so I went to Kempton's office. He had quit his practice to become the Associate Medical Director of Maritime Medical Care Inc. I appeared in his new office in the Lord Nelson Building, and he waved me in to be seated. He could tell there was something drastically wrong. I told him what had happened.

"So what do you want to do about it, Billy?"

"I haven't a clue," I replied dryly. "That's why I'm here to see you."

"Are you prepared for a lengthy fight?"

"I have no alternative."

"OK, then. Let's fight." He wasn't buying the first interviewer's results. "I'm going to arrange for you to be re-tested."

Two weeks later I got a call from the office of a psychiatrist named Sol Hirsch. I went in hung over, and close to a nervous breakdown. An immaculate dresser, Hirsch struck me as a very pleasant man.

"Billy, you seem to have quite a problem," he said, still standing. "We'll have to see what we can do about this." I felt I could relax with him, and we talked about all kinds of things in the course of an hour: growing up in poverty, my personal life as a kid, but mostly about my relationships as an adult. When I walked out I thought he would be fair.

A week went by. Hirsch's secretary phoned to make an appointment to see both myself and Carol. I wasn't expecting this, but we went in. Hirsch spoke to us casually for several minutes and then he took Carol into another office and interviewed her for about an hour. When they came back, he complimented me on my lovely wife. Carol turned to me and said: "There's nothing he doesn't know about you and me, since the day we met!"

"In that case, he should be able to write a good book!" I said, thinking about our loving and hot relationship when we were single.

Two weeks after the appointment with Hirsch I got a call to show up for still another appointment with a psychologist at the Victoria General Hospital psych ward. At eight pm on a Wednesday, I walked in to my fourth interview. Dressed casually this time, I took a seat in Lynn Ross's office. My first female interviewer was in her mid-thirties, a bit taller than me, and very attractive. With high cheekbones, a peaches-and-cream complexion, and just a touch of red lipstick, she looked a lot like Carol!

After going through some of the usual questions, she gave me an inkblot test. Next, she showed me some pictures and asked what was wrong with them. One was a hunter and his dog who were walking through the snow, but there were no footprints for the dog. Then she gave me a set of blocks and, showing me a picture of a design, she asked me to arrange them to match. When I asked if I could have another ten or fifteen seconds, she said the time was up. I was frustrated because I hadn't finished, and then noticed she was writing a lot in her notebook.

Two and a half hours had flown by!

It was ten-thirty at night. When I asked her how I did, she said things went well, and that Dr. Hirsch would be in touch with me.

Three weeks later, Hirsch called and said he wanted me to see a psychiatrist named Edwin Rosenberg at Camp Hill Hospital. The appointment was already set up for the next day, which was a Saturday. When I went to the Outpatients section of the psychiatric ward, there was no receptionist so I found his office and knocked on his door. A short man—my height—with dark bushy hair and thick horn-rimmed glasses greeted me at the door. In contrast to my dark business suit, he was wearing a checkered lumberjack shirt, grey slacks, and dark grey Hush Puppies®. Rosenberg offered me a chair in a manner that was both friendly and businesslike.

"I know why you're here," he said. "I've read Dr. Hirsch's report."

I reached up to feel the cigar that was sticking out of the lapel pocket of my suit.

"Why did you feel your cigar just now?"

Knowing I had to be careful what I said, I froze up and remained silent. Finally I answered, "I don't know why."

"Do you want to smoke it?"

I knew it wouldn't be right to smoke the cigar in his office, so I said, "No."

"Then why did you feel it?" he persisted.

A bundle of nerves, and not knowing what to say, I looked him in the eye for what must have been a minute. I figured the best I could do was to get up and walk out.

Then, out of the blue, I started to shoot with him. "If I fail this interview," I said, "I'm going to give you this cigar."

Rosenberg's brow wrinkled and he looked at me funny. "If I fail you, you're going to give *me* this cigar? Shouldn't it be the other way around?"

"No," I said. "You see, this cigar is filled with TNT. If you fail me, I'm going to give you this cigar and blow your fuckin' head off!" I said this as if I were dead serious.

Rosenberg started to laugh, and then I laughed with him. After that, we got along well for the remaining half-hour.

When I left his office I was feeling good but then one day followed the other and I became anxious again. This endless succession of shrinks was killing Carol and me. Maybe I really *was* crazy! Maybe they were building an airtight case to not only remove me from the force once and for all, but to lock me up in the loony bin. It was all I could do to get through another boring day at work feeling useless—delivering mail, running errands, and writing tickets.

Two weeks later, Dr. Hirsch's secretary phoned and asked me to go to the Nova Scotia Hospital that afternoon. When I arrived, two doctors dressed in white smocks casually led me to one of the wards and introduced me to some of the patients who were sitting around chatting. Two of them were male officers from out of town: one RCMP and one Canadian Army officer. Then the doctors led me down the hall and I sat in a reception area. What the hell was that all about? I wondered. Are they getting ready to commit me?

A doctor came out to usher me into an exam room.

"Do you drink very much?" he said.

"Yeah, at times. It's a bit heavy lately because of all this. My nerves are shot. I don't know how much more I can take. Every time I turn around, someone's calling me to see some goddamn head shrinker."

He was the first professional to suggest I might be an excessive drinker.

The following week, Hirsch's secretary phoned to say he had just sent his report to Dr. Hayes. Kemp told me the findings: I was mentally stable to carry a firearm! The report had already been sent to the Police Department. A huge weight lifted from my shoulders. I felt almost giddy.

I drove straight to the Chief's office and, as I was standing at attention, he said, "Our office in Ottawa is not acknowledging your testing. They are abiding by the first test. You cannot be issued a firearm."

The Chief's words hit me right in my gut. After all I'd been through, I'd had the best in the country testing me and they weren't going to recognize the results? I simply turned, exited, drove home, and poured myself a few drinks at the kitchen table. When Carol walked in, she said, "You must be celebrating"— and then she saw my face. I filled her in and she sat down and said, "Now *I* need a drink."

Later that evening I phoned Kempton to tell him the latest story of how I was getting the shaft.

"There's no question in my mind," he said. "They're giving you the royal run-around. If they take away your gun, that's the end of your career. What's a guy with a Grade Five education going to do?"

When I didn't respond, he said, "You know what, Bill? You and I are going to fight this."

I could always count on Kemp.

The next day (it was in late November, 1972) he unexpectedly appeared in Shed 23. "Where in the hell can I find Alex Taylor?" Kemp boomed. I had rarely seen him so angry. I said the Chief was in his office, and showed him the way.

Kemp strode into Alex's office and said, "I have a patient who has been put through a lot of unnecessary stress, and I want it stopped, *now*."

The Chief knew who he was talking about, and said he'd get back to him within a week. One week later, on December sixth, he sent Kemp a letter informing him that a decision had been made to refer the matter to the head office at the Department of National Health and Welfare in Ottawa.

Since the Department didn't have anyone qualified to make such an assessment, they had to select an outside assessor. Two months crawled by.

During those two months I drank myself into oblivion. Carol and I didn't fight or argue, because we didn't speak! I wasn't in the mood to talk with this thing hanging over my head. The most difficult period for us was Christmas and New Year's, but we managed to put on a front for the sake of the kids.

On a Friday evening in mid-March 1973, Dr. Kovacs called me from his home, saying he'd like to see me at his ninth floor office in the Medical Arts Building at nine o'clock the following morning. He wouldn't tell me his findings on the phone. I figured it must be bad.

The next morning, I wrote a letter to the Chief: "I hereby tender my resignation as a police officer (Sergeant) effective the above date. Yours Truly, William S. Taylor (Sgt.)." When Carol saw the letter she said, "See the doctor before you turn that in."

"Fuck Dr. Kovacs, fuck the department, and fuck you!" I yelled, and stormed out.

I was driving to work when I pulled up to a red light at Robie Street and Spring Garden Road. Looking across the street at the Halifax Professional Centre I said, "To hell with it," parked, and rode the elevator up to the ninth floor. It was around nine-thirty and the floor was dark. I walked down the corridor looking for the room number. When I turned right, I noticed a pale light shining outside an office. I went over to the open door and walked in. A man was sitting behind a desk, working by the light of a lamp. His white hair was standing up straight; Coke bottle glasses sat at the end of his nose. He was wearing a blue shirt with no necktie, wrinkled brown baggy pants, and brownish shoes that hadn't seen a lick of polish since they were new.

Judging from his casual dress, I became suspicious. He didn't *look* like a doctor! But then I remembered it was Saturday and no one else was around. He must have come in wearing his putter-about-the-house clothes—much like I dressed when I was off-duty.

For this guy to come in on his day off, I told myself, he must have one hell of a lot of bad news to tell me.

"Mr. Taylor," he whispered. "Come in, come in."

What the fuck is he whispering for? There's no one else in the building!

I sat across from him. Leaning towards me, he said, "Do you know what?"

"I don't know anything."

"You know, somebody's crazy!"

I sat there looking at him, stone-faced.

"Somebody's crazy, but it's not you. In fact, you're the *last* person I want to see. The people that put you through this would have to be crazy. I hope you're going to sue them."

"No, I'm not going to sue anybody," I said. "I just want to go back to work."

"If you sue them, we'll all be there for you in court."

"No, I just want to get this over with, and be a cop." And with that, I got up and walked out of his office. I felt terrific, but I wanted to get revenge—the Taylor way.

As I pulled into the driveway, Carol came out and stood on the doorstep. She could tell it was good news. She ran over and hugged and kissed me, and we had a wonderful weekend together—me, Carol, and my forty-ouncer.

Back at the office on Monday morning, the Chief called me in to say how glad he was that I won. It was what the guys had been saying: they knew I would win. But where were they when I needed them? The Chief gave me my gun back and apologized.

After a moment of silence, he said in a slow, low voice: "Sergeant, do you intend to sue over this matter?"

I took my time answering, noting that this was the second time in three days I had been asked that question. Finally, I said, "No. It is not my intention to sue anyone." But the way I said it left room for interpretation.

"Well, then, is there anything I can do?"

"Yes, as a matter of fact, I'd like a letter of apology."

"That's no problem, Sergeant."

"But I'd like it from the head man," I said unexpectedly. "Director General Donald N. Cassidy."

"Don't do that, Billy. Don't ask Cassidy. It wasn't his doing. I'll apologize to you, but don't ask him."

At that moment I felt powerful. 'Here I am with my hands around everybody's throat, and all I have to do is squeeze. God, do I ever feel good!'

I was so full of hate and revenge—and alcohol—I *insisted* on an apology from Cassidy. I was getting even, but it wasn't just about having my gun taken away and the psychological testing. It was about everything else that had happened in my life, and now Cassidy was the one who was going to pay.

A month later, Cassidy's letter of apology arrived. Now, *that* was a victory! Poor Billy Taylor had forced Ottawa to its knees. Little did I know how much my grandstanding would damage my career. One sentence from the letter stuck in my head: "I hope some day Sergeant Taylor will see the light."

Some years later, I saw Cassidy on Parliament Hill and he didn't speak to me—nor did he for the rest of my police career.

The last time I saw Director General Donald N. Cassidy (not in photograph) was at this ceremony to honour fallen officers, on Parliament Hill, 1984. I'm the short guy in the centre.
Photographer unknown.

About a week later I dropped by to thank Kemp for standing by me through this ordeal. He was pleased that I had won my case, but he was reserved. As I was leaving his office we shook hands. He held on to my hand saying, "A word of advice, Billy. You've won the battle but I doubt you've won the war. Now your name is circled in red. You're sitting on a powder keg. Watch your step, and watch whose toes you step on."

I said to myself, 'I'll step on anyone's toes I feel like stepping on, dammit! As for that powder keg, I just need to catch whoever's trying to light the damn fuse.'

Kemp's warning went right over my head.

Years later, he and I were sitting in the family room of his comfortable home, reminiscing. He noted that I had dropped out of sight soon after he received that wrestling picture of me—the one I sent to show him what a big cheese I was. The psycho testing was the next time he'd heard from me.

"That's when you came back," he recalled. "I've often thought that was just a smokescreen. They seemed to have made up their minds what they were going to do, and they were using that psychological testing as an excuse to get rid of you." After a moment's pause, he said "You were a thorn in their side. You had a lot to say, and you were honest."

Then Kemp remembered the time I put the squeeze on three senior port cops who had outfitted their homes with wood panelling that had supposedly been damaged in handling.

"You went to a Customs informant who was a friend of yours," Kemp recalled. "He said they'd have to pay the duty since it was an import. You went up to those guys and told them they'd have to either pay the duty, or return the panelling that was up on their walls! They ended up paying the duty."

No wonder the people at the top were trying to get rid of me.

Soon after the Port Days banquet was held at the Hotel Nova Scotian, a senior shipping official called to let me know what he had overheard.

"Certain politicians and Longshoremen's Union officials suggested to Chief Taylor that you should be removed from the force," he said. "Alex's reply was: 'No one tells me or even suggests who I should fire or hire. The day that happens, I quit.'"

God bless Alex. There was never a For Sale sign on him.

9. CROOKS WHERE YOU LEAST EXPECT THEM

Back on the beat, everyone knew I had failed the psychological testing. The waterfront workers would holler "fruitcake" and "cracker box" as I walked by. They thought I had something missing upstairs. It made me feel uneasy. I started to consider moving out west where I could start over. At the Criminal Identification course in Ottawa two years earlier, I had struck up a friendship with Bob Shortridge, the Inspector of the Vancouver Port Police. Since then, when I'd phone the Vancouver Port Police on business I usually ended up talking to Bob. Each time, he'd remind me there was a job for me out there as his Ident. man.

It was time for a change.

On November 1, 1973 I submitted my transfer request to Alex who forwarded it to the Director General in Ottawa. I didn't hear back and, after a few weeks, let it drop. They would have just told me that my request was under consideration—a polite way of saying it had found a permanent home in a filing cabinet. I figured my letter to Cassidy was coming back to haunt me so I decided to grin and bear it. After about six months of taunts and jeers—which I had learned to live with as a kid—I began to feel comfortable on the waterfront again.

It was during a nighttime patrol in January that I squared off with "Bright Eyes" Freddie, which is where I began my story. Once I had him handcuffed I realized this wasn't going to look good. When I first saw the light under the boxcar, I should have backed away and called in. If something had happened to me, no one would know where to look. I'd handled this like a rookie.

I called for backup, and a squad car hauled Freddie into the station along with the cartons of footwear he had scattered on the ground. I went inside Shed 22. Tony, the watchman, was watching TV in the rest area. In his mid-fifties, Tony was a well-educated man who was a chronic alcoholic. I told him that goods from his shed had been stolen, and it caught him off guard. With thousands of boxes in the shed stacked to the rafters, there was no way he could tell where the boxes had come from. The only way we were going to be able to prove the theft was with proper documentation.

It took two weeks to gather the paperwork. Tony was served with a summons to appear in court. Since the goods had been under his care and custody, he was the prime candidate to testify. But I had failed to take a written statement from him prior to the court date. On the big day, Tony showed up in a suit and tie which seemed rather odd. When he took the stand he looked uneasy, glancing to the left and right—not at all like the watchman I knew who was always at home wherever he was.

The Crown prosecutor showed Tony the documentation for the cartons of footwear. "How can I tell from what's on this paper whether or not that cargo was in Shed 22?" Tony asked.

Asked if the carton numbers in the documentation matched the ones found, Tony said vaguely, "I don't know, I didn't look at the numbers." The more questions were asked, he kept answering, "Don't know...Can't answer that."

Tony had caved; our case was toast.

Then it was my turn. The defence lawyer grilled me on my intentions when I was pointing my gun at Bright Eyes. "Had the accused come towards me with the hook, I would have shot him," I stated matter-of-factly.

"To kill?"

"Yes, sir," I said curtly.

"No further questions, Your Honour."

Bright Eyes never took the stand. During his summary, the defence lawyer grabbed onto the weak link in the case, like a dog with a bone: "Who actually owns the goods?" he challenged. "How do we know they came from Pier 22? The watchman, who has sole custody and control, doesn't know. My client was in the area at the time, but no one saw him come out of the shed. Admittedly, he was intoxicated. When he looked up and saw someone in front of him he was terrified. He took out his cotton hook to defend himself."

Judge Eric D. Murray was presiding. Judge Murray spent a lot of his spare time at the piers and in the sheds because he was fascinated by the waterfront. I had seen him walking through the sheds on Sundays, sometimes with his young grandson, talking to the longshoremen, and marvelling at the volumes of cargo stacked all the way to the roof. Judge Murray knew that the import-export trade is vital to Canada's economy, and that it was vulnerable to the threat posed by the theft of cargo.

The Judge motioned to Bright Eyes to stand before him. Looking at him squarely, he said: "I find you not guilty."

Bright Eyes and his partner in crime Jake were snickering at me as they walked out of the courtroom. The Judge told the prosecutor and me to convene in his chambers.

As soon as we were seated, he lit into me: "You didn't do your bloody homework, Sergeant Taylor. Next time you come into my court, make sure you have the proper documentation, and a half-credible witness—not a half-drunk watchman. This sort of theft is serious, but you've got to make your case. If you had presented a case here today I was prepared to sentence this guy to eight years."

I felt about two feet tall when I walked out. The only good news was that the defence lawyer hadn't questioned my judgment when I said I would have shot to kill, nor did he question my sanity. At the office I told Alex what happened. He sat behind his desk looking glum. We agreed that Tony had either been threatened or he was getting a kickback—or both.

"These goddamn watchmen," Alex finally blurted out. He rose from his chair and started to pace. "I want a dossier on every one of them on this waterfront. That includes what these guys eat for lunch, even what time they take a shit. I want everything on them!"

"But there must be fifty or more, sir," I protested. "*All* of them?"

Alex stopped in his tracks and, stabbing his index finger at the air, turned to me. "All of them," he said firmly. "Every last one of 'em. Now, why are you standing there, Sergeant? Get to it!"

I was pissed off. I thought Alex was doing this to punish me for my incompetence. He was turning me into a paper-pushing jockey cop, and I'm not a paper man. But I did as I was told. I started out collecting information on fifteen watchmen—what kind of car they drove, where they lived, and some of their habits. We were on the look-out for gambling, drugs, alcohol, and lifestyles that were too lavish for a watchman's means.

About two weeks later, Alex called me into his office to ask about a watchman named Stubby. This guy was a peddler in the summertime—the slow season for the cargo trade. Alex wanted me to check him out and find out what he sells, and where he sells it. I asked around and found out that Stubby was peddling pots, pans, clothing, shoes, and household appliances. He took his wares outside the city and hawked them on backcountry roads in the Valley and up the Eastern Shore. I also found out that his prices were much lower than anywhere else in town—even the Sears bargain basement store.

When I reported this to Alex, he said, "Well, I wouldn't exactly call this guy an Avon lady. Stake him out."

I knew that a stakeout at the pier would get burnt so instead I parked an unmarked car across from Stubby's house on Cunard Street. Since he worked the night shift I expected to see him come home between six o'clock and seven o'clock in the morning. I sat there at my post in the dark with a pair of high-powered binoculars. On the fourth morning, Stubby drove up in his bluish green Chrysler, got out, opened the trunk, and removed several brown paper shopping bags. I found it odd that each of the bags was creased down the middle. What kind of a store would bag their goods in used sacks?

My plan was to continue the stakeout to see if he had a storage unit where he was stashing the stuff, but Alex was ready to pounce. "Get a search warrant and knock him off now," he said abruptly.

The next morning, three officers and I paid Stubby a visit. He answered the door with his usual smile, greeting us with a pleasant voice. His paunchy, round face looked like a basketball. A heavy-set man in his mid-forties, Stubby was wearing a dip hat (like the TV detectives used to wear) and a long brown overcoat. His face flushed, he showed us inside. Right away we noticed padlocks on the doors of two of the front rooms.

"We'd like to get in these rooms, Stubby," I said. "You want to open them up?"

Without hesitating he replied, "My wife's got the keys and she's not home." One of my men left and came back a few minutes later with a crowbar. Stubby suddenly found the keys and pulled off the padlocks. I opened one of the doors onto a bizarre scene. There were six electric eggbeaters, twelve blenders, several toasters and hair dryers, and assorted electrical appliances on the window sills, tables, floor, and closet shelves. Later I tallied about $5,000 worth of goods in that room.

"OK, Stubby," I said. "Don't start telling me your wife has been doing her Christmas shopping. You're being charged with possession of stolen goods."

We brought him into the station and took a statement. In court, we could only charge Stubby for stealing goods that had been shipped recently, since only they could be traced to the previous owners: four blenders, two irons, and five eggbeaters. He was fined $1,000 and dismissed from his watchman's job. I tried to turn him into an informant, but couldn't. He wouldn't budge. Either Stubby knew too much, or he was so sore at being caught he was dead set against giving me the satisfaction.

Stubby's arrest showed that our watchman dossiers were starting to pay off. We were beginning to think they might even be the key to unravelling the organized theft rings. These guys were supposed to be the guardians of the goods—the cops of the sheds! We had assumed they were trustworthy because of their position. We felt like dopes for not seeing what was going on right under our noses.

The same week we nabbed Stubby, Alex told me to check on some copper ingots that had gone missing from Shed 34.

I headed over and found the head checker who had made the call. He pointed at a pile of ingots on the track side: "Three ingots are missing from that pile," he said. "I'm reporting it so no one blames me for a wrong count."

A copper ingot is not all that easy to pinch. It's four feet long, six inches high, pyramid shaped, rounded on the ends—and weighs 300 pounds! Ingots are a dull brownish orange, and have a number stamped on the bottom. There were nine ingots to a pallet which were cross-piled four high, and there were fifty piles—a total of 1,800 bars. Three were missing from the far corner of the top pallet. That would be easy to miss.

I began compiling a list of all the watchmen, longshoremen, and checkers who had worked between Friday at five o'clock pm (the last time the ingots were seen) and eight o'clock Monday morning. There were 125 suspects. Since the thief must have had a way to move them off the premises, I checked the parking permit ledgers and discovered that several half-ton trucks had been on the lot over the weekend. Next I looked up the dossiers of the watchmen who had been on shift. A policeman told me he thought the Sunday watchman had come to work in a pick-up truck. That would have been James.

I knew James—well enough to know that he was always hard up for money. I headed to his house in Dartmouth. Since it was eleven o'clock in the morning, he'd be sleeping off the night shift. I knocked and he came to the door with only his pants on. Well built, he was of medium height and light skinned. James's sharp nose was his most noticeable feature.

We stood in his brightly lit kitchen. After the customary small talk I got down to business. "James, did you drive a half-ton truck to work within the last few nights?"

"Yes. My car broke down and I couldn't get anyone to fix it," he answered, almost mechanically.

"Which night was this?"

"Sunday."

"So who'd you get the truck from?" I asked, casually.

"Some guy up the street."

I pressed him and James said he didn't know the guy's name. He added, "I asked if he could give me a lift to work and he said, what the hell, go ahead and take the truck." His voice was shrill and shaky.

It bothered me that James couldn't name the owner of the truck. I noticed how nervous he was, shifting from leg to leg, drumming his fingers on the counter top, and not once looking me in the eye. He finally slumped down into his chair at the kitchen table and stared straight ahead at the floor.

After a brief silence I thanked him for his help. "If you need anything else, don't hesitate to come here or see me at work," he offered. I checked the car rental shops to see if any of the workers had been in over the weekend. James's name appeared on Hertz's rental records. So he borrowed a truck, and rented one too?

After suppertime, another investigator and I caught James by surprise at work. I flashed him the truck rental papers.

"Do you have lots of money to rent a truck?" I asked. "Why couldn't you have just taken a bus to work? How come you didn't walk or hitchhike? Why did you rent a truck and borrow another truck the same night?"

I walked up close to him and asked, "Where are the ingots?"

"I don't want to talk to you anymore," he mumbled, walking away. "I've got nothing more to say."

"James, can I see you in the washroom for a minute?" I said politely, figuring I wouldn't have to be so careful how I spoke to him if we were alone.

He was a wrestling fan who never missed a match. He had seen me referee often enough to know I was a mean sonofabitch. Inside, I convinced him to spill the beans.

When we came out of the washroom, James walked up to the other investigator. He told him when and how he stole the ingots, and who he sold them to.

James had pulled it off by himself. Late Sunday night he drove the Hertz truck into the shed, closed the door, used a forklift to load the ingots, and parked the truck in the lot. After his shift he drove to a scrap dealer in Dartmouth, where he sold them.

We took a statement from James, obtained a search warrant, and paid the scrap dealer a visit. The ingots were in the basement. The dealer was going to cut them up and sell them piecemeal. We arrested him and he pled guilty in court. Judge Murray sentenced the bugger to pay a $2,500 fine. As for James, he served nine months in the Halifax Correctional Centre. In his closing remarks, the Judge said, "It warrants serving time because this person was in a position of trust. Let this be a lesson to waterfront workers that we will not tolerate the theft of cargo at the Port of Halifax."

First it was Stubby, and now James. Watchmen had a miserable job, working twelve-hour shifts in those cold, dirty, rat-infested sheds. They had a hell of a lot of responsibility, and very little support to stay on the straight and narrow. They were paid eight dollars an hour, compared to twenty dollars an hour for policemen. Since we knew how common it was for cops to take bribes, it made even more sense for *these* guys to be on the take. And once they got started, it was too profitable to stop.

Not only was the temptation great, they were outnumbered. I could picture the checkers and freight handlers going up to them and saying, "Listen you fucker, you just try stopping us, and a goddamn machine will run right over you or a set of forks (from a forklift) will go right through you." It's no wonder most of them caved. If I'm going to let *them* steal, they figured, I might as well get something out of this too.

Fred Smith was an exception. A balding, heavyset man about my height, Fred was in his mid-seventies at the time and was working for Furnace, Withy & Co. He wore thick black glasses, a red-and-black checkered hunting jacket, heavy work clothes and a salt-and-pepper cap, and walked with a cane. He was assigned to Pier 3 where he oversaw the unloading and storage of manufactured goods from England: chinaware, footwear, clothing, automobiles, steel, and liquor. Fred always helped us when he could, calling in if one of the shed doors was up or if anything needed attention. A few days after the copper ingot case, I stopped in on him..

As I approached Pier 3 North I took a deep breath. The smell of coconut fibre mixed with the salt air told me that door mats had been unloaded that day from the Far East.

Fred was sitting in the stevedore's lunchroom watching TV when I walked in. The word had spread fast about Stubby and James and, all of a sudden, I wasn't too popular among the watchmen. I tried to strike up a conversation but Fred gave me the cold shoulder. Finally he said: "Oh. So this is how you're repaying us." Usually friendly, his tone of voice was bitter. "So now you're going to turn on old Fred! Is that it?"

I knew Fred fairly well, and his remark caught me off guard. "These guys doing the stealing are taking the bread and butter off your table," I said. "They're jeopardizing your job. It's just like crooked cops; they ruin it for the rest of us."

He just sat there staring at the baseball game.

"Any watchman that's not stealing has nothing to worry about," I said flatly. "You people are in a position of trust. You're like cops, only you don't have the powers that we do."

"Well, we'll see," is all he said. It took Fred about a month before he started to come around. He still wouldn't squeal on the other watchmen or longshoremen, but I could tell he appreciated my efforts to nail the thieving bastards. There were several watchmen like Fred: honest, reliable, hard-working guys. Many of them were disabled and had come to the waterfront years ago from the Bill Lynch Circus. That's where I first met Bingo Risser, Jimmer Walsh, and Hot Dog Lohnes—and now, they were all cargo watchmen!

Jimmer had only one arm. He lost the other as a very young boy when he ran in front of a man who was firing a shotgun in a domestic dispute. It blasted his arm off to the elbow. In the circus he used to give piggy-back rides to his brother-in-law, Jigger, who had no legs.

By the time our paths crossed on the waterfront, Jimmer had been working as a watchman most of his life. Although he was nearly blind from cataracts, at sixty he was still working for Saguenay Shipping in Shed 36. Jimmer's son-in-law would drop him off around five-thirty pm and I would bring him into the shed and position him where he would "watch" the cargo during the six to ten shift. He spent the rest of his shift in the shed lunchroom. Saguenay's Captain Bohlman (the shore captain), a few other cops, and myself were the only ones who knew about Jimmer's eyesight.

Since we were starting to close in on the watchmen, I figured it was a good time to go chew the fat with Larry, my prime informant. Larry was the one who gave me the scoop on the cops who had been stealing cargo from Shed 20, and ever since then I could pretty much depend on him for good information. This particular night Larry was working at Pier 21. I caught a whiff of a sweet smell as I approached the shed. That meant that raw rubber and tea had just landed from India. Two-inch cockroaches had infested both this building and the administration building at Pier 19, and now their relatives had made the long trip to join them.

After exchanging greetings with Larry, I started right in. "You know goddamn well what's going on here with the theft of cargo. It's a lot bigger than what you've been telling me."

"I can't tell you that," he said offhandedly. "I wouldn't know what you want to know anyway." And then he let slip: "You'd have to talk to someone like Stanley."

Now, that was an angle I hadn't thought of. Stanley wasn't too swift, but he had been around longer than most. As I was turning over the idea in my mind, Larry said, "Oops. Don't tell Stanley I ever mentioned his name."

"Did I ever mention your name to anyone?" I replied.

"I know, Billy. You'd never say anything, for God sakes."

I thanked him for his time and headed out. Stanley was one of the original watchmen when I first came to work at the Port. He was a smallish man—about 5' 5" and 110 pounds—with dark, bushy eyebrows. He was always dressed in a white shirt and tie, and gave the impression he had a low IQ. Back at the office I read through his dossier. Outside the waterfront his only involvement was as a churchwarden.[7] I knew that Stanley picked up worthless junk from the warehouse floor on Fridays to take home—a broken piece of cargo, nuts and bolts, a discarded pen. It was the closest he could come to stealing, and he used to enjoy bragging about it as if he was one of the boys, as if he was brave enough to steal like the stevedores. He was a harmless, frail guy who wanted to be tough. This was his best shot at being like them.

---

7 A lay representative of a parish.

On Friday at five-thirty I parked between Shed 36 and Shed 40 so I could see who was coming out of both ends of the building. When Stanley walked by I asked him to come over and sit in the front seat of the police car because I wanted to have a word with him. I knew Stanley had my next lead and I was prepared to squeeze him if I had to. He probably thought I was going to give him a lift home.

"Stanley, I've brought you into the car so no one will see you," I said seriously. "I want to check your lunch pail." I grabbed it from him and opened it. Inside was a kid's wristwatch and a fountain pen.

"I found them in the shed," Stanley said promptly, with a hint of pride.

"I don't doubt it, but it's still cargo."

"I guess so," he answered, not having a clue where this was headed.

"If it's cargo, you're under arrest for theft." He looked at me blankly, not believing his ears.

"Remember the watchman with the copper ingots?" I prodded. "He did jail time. Now, Stanley, do you want to go to jail?"

He was speechless. No one had ever done this to him before.

"Now Stanley, you know what's going on at the upper levels on this waterfront, and that's what you're going to tell me."

"I don't know anything." Stanley started to panic. "I tell you what. Let's make a deal. I'll take these back and leave them in the shed." He grabbed hold of the lunch pail.

"No. I've already seized them. It's too late to take them back. And furthermore, if you can't come up with some good top-level information for me, I'm going to tell them at your church that they have a fucking thief for a warden."

Stanley burst into tears. He sat there sobbing, his shoulders jerking forward, his hands brushing at his eyes. I felt like a piece of shit. This was not my usual MO, picking on people like Stanley, but I was desperate to find out how to get to the heart of the theft rings. Finally, I said, "I'll give you one week and if you don't tell me something that's going on at the top level—and I'm not talking about longshoremen and checkers, I'm talking about the boss level—then I'm going to charge you with theft of cargo and I'm going to tell your church." He was crying his heart out when I handed him his lunch pail and reached over to open the passenger door. "Now, get out. I'll be back in a week."

Four days later one of the cops told me that Stanley was looking for me. I went to Pier 39 and as I walked past him to avoid being seen together in public, he said, "This afternoon, at four o'clock, there's a truckload of plywood leaving Pier 21." I nodded discreetly and kept on walking but Stanley ran after me, saying "OK Billy? OK? Hey, hey?"

"Yeah. OK, Stan."

And then he ran in front of me. "Did I do a good job, Billy?" he asked eagerly. "Hey?"

"Stanley, ya did real fine." He looked as pleased as if I had handed him a million dollars.

At three o'clock we set up a stakeout on Pier 21. From my unmarked car I could see the entries to both Pier 21 and Pier 20. I put four port cops in two marked police cars on Water Street and Terminal Road. All I told them was that we were going to intercept a truck. I didn't want everyone on the waterfront to know our plan.

At four o'clock sharp, a green five-ton flatbed truck rolled away from Pier 21. It was loaded with plywood, strapped down, and tarped. As it turned onto Marginal Road to head toward the city, I radioed a description of the truck to the Port Police cars, and added "1093". That was code for "Set up a roadblock." Five minutes later they radioed me back "1060", code for "Negative". That meant the driver's license and dock receipts were in order. Oh. So Stanley must have been feeding me a line of crap just to get me off his case! I wanted to drive over to Shed 39 and do some serious damage to the little prick. Meanwhile, my men were waiting for instructions.

"Give me the info on the driver," I barked into the mike. "I'm going to run a 10 29 (criminal record check) on this guy." The minute I heard the driver's name I knew we were on the right track. He was a two-time loser the city detectives had been chasing for months, a hood who'd been convicted twice for receiving and selling stolen goods. I told the officer to bring the subject to the police station.

When I questioned the driver, he didn't know who had hired him to deliver the goods. He was just bringing them to a meeting point at Upper Water Street and Cornwallis Street. I could tell I wasn't going to get anywhere with him, not until I brought the city dicks in on it. They had been eager to get this guy and he was terrified of them, but I wanted to keep control of the case. I stationed two of my men with the driver, saying I might need to use him as a witness rather than charge him with possession. Then I went to talk to the manager who had signed for the release of the plywood.

At about five-fifty pm I knocked on the door of Harry Smith's apartment. The manager of a stevedoring company, Harry had a sharp, pasty white face, thinning hair, and brown glasses. He came to the door in a white shirt and light brown suit pants. Harry looked as though he had just lost his best friend.

"I expected you would be here," he said right off the bat.

I was baffled. Why would he be expecting me? I hadn't called. As I stood there trying to think of what to say, he added, "I guess you got me."

Now I'm thinking, OK. I got you. What the hell are you talking about? Then it clicked. This little sonofabitch is in on it! An informant of mine, Harry had blown the whistle on a lot of guys, but I never suspected he was working both ends against the middle. So as not to give away my ignorance, I said, "You are under arrest for theft. Now listen to what I have to read you," and I read him his rights. I gave him the choice of coming to the station in handcuffs, or riding in the passenger seat without a scene. He put on his trench coat and followed me to the car. Because of our informant relationship, at the station I had another investigator question him and take his statement. On the way back to his place we stopped for coffee and sat sipping it in the car.

"Your wife works with you," I said between mouthfuls.

"What's she got to do with this?" Harry cried.

"The reason I'm taking you home is I'm going to arrest her as an accessory to theft."

Harry nearly leapt through the roof. "She's got nothing to do with this. She doesn't know anything about it!"

I told him I wanted to know what's going on at the top levels on the waterfront. "You know because you're part of it."

"I can't tell you that, Billy." He was pleading with me. "Besides, you wouldn't want to know."

"Try me."

"There's no way I can tell you that."

So I started the car and put it into gear. "OK. If that's the way you want it, I'm going to arrest your wife. I'll drag her out of the fucking house in handcuffs, screaming."

Now bawling, Harry yelled, "This is nothing more than blackmail! Billy, I never thought you were like this."

"Harry, this is the best deal you're gonna get today: if you give me information, your wife stays out of this."

We sat in silence for two or three minutes, and Harry started telling me the names of companies and port workers, how documentation was altered and forged, and how cargo was moved around. Perfectly good cargo was claimed to be water damaged, and sold off. Cargo that was reported short landed was, in fact, here. Stevedores would give their friends' names to the timekeeper, so it looked like they were there when they were absent. The paymaster would hand out the cheques, and the guys would give them to their buddies. The ships' chandlers would buy a can of milk for fifty cents, sell it to the ship's Captain for two dollars, and get a kickback. They were doing this with all the food, shipboard equipment, and supplies.

Then I asked Harry about the Rat's MO. This was a guy who had driven the cops crazy for some time. We knew he was robbing the place blind, but we could never catch up with him. Harry told me he had a stash of cargo hidden among the gear that was used to load and unload cargo—pallets, forklifts, rope, and cables. Apparently, he'd hide the cargo he was stealing under the seats of the forklift and bring it to his hiding place at Pier 22 Upper. He said the Rat probably had $5,000 worth of stuff stored there at the time.

Harry warned me not to use this information because it goes too high up. If I did, people with influence and power would get rid of me overnight. They would make sure I woke up with another job in another city. "Everyone on the waterfront hates your guts, Billy," he said, "including most of the guys on the police force. You're beat before you start just with your own guys and the workforce here, never mind what the top guys would do to you."

"The reason I'm hated is I don't back down from anybody," I explained. "No one owns me or pushes me around, and I don't take bribes. I won't even take a free cup of coffee or a penny book of matches. No one's got me in their pocket."

When I dropped Harry off at his house he said, "I've told you all I know." I said I wouldn't mention anything to his wife. After all, a deal's a deal.

Harry was fined $2,500 and he resigned from his position as company manager, but I think his wife served a heavier sentence. The next morning she showed up for work just like any other day, and had to ask around the office to find out why Harry wasn't there. It was pitiful. Harry had kept a lady friend on the side. Keeping her comfortable was part of his reason for stealing, and probably why he didn't want his wife dragged into the mess.

Now I was ready to catch the Rat. After midnight I put on coveralls, went to Pier 22 Upper and moved the pallets around until I saw where they had been tunnelled out to create a storage area. In the centre towards the back was a room full of wrenches, tools, shoes, clothing, and household appliances. I knew this was too hot for me to pursue by myself so I fed the information to our department through an outside source.

On Monday morning I looked up the Rat, a little nervous guy. "Billy, why would someone be in the old grain gallery at Pier 22 Upper watching the shed?" he asked.

"Maybe he's there to make sure nobody is going to steal one of your pallets." The Rat broke up when he heard this, and slapped me on the back.

"Taylor, one thing I like is a cop with a sense of humour. Jeez, I love that." And all this time, I'm wondering, how did he know a cop was up there just two hours into the stakeout? This guy must be well connected!

Since the stakeout was burnt, our guys just turned over the goods to Customs, and the Rat went off scot-free. Many years later, he was charged with committing arson at his place of business outside of town.

Around this time, an informant handed me a classified document I wasn't supposed to see. It said there had been a large increase in cargo theft at the Halterm Container Terminal, but the National Harbours Board Police had received very few reports. There was a graph that compared the value of goods reported stolen to the value of goods that had been recovered. The ratio was about four to one. Interesting that so little had been found!

Right after the incident with the Rat, a new man came onto my shift—Eric Mott. He was stocky—240 pounds and 6' 1"—and cocky. Eric seemed to think he was better and smarter than everyone else, and when I found out he had been a Mountie, that explained at least part of it. He was probably thinking 'You guys are only port cops, and I'm a Mountie.' I picked up on his snooty attitude right away. To me, he was "Florence". I always used to come up with nicknames for people I met—a throwback from the wrestling business.

Born in Dartmouth, Eric had joined the RCMP at nineteen, went through his basic training in Regina, and was stationed in Watrous, Saskatchewan. Joining my shift at twenty-five, after having worn the Mountie's red serge, must have been a bit of a come down for him. Right from the start, he was all business. He never mixed with the rest of the guys.

It didn't take long for Eric to form an opinion of me, especially after talking with the other members. Later he told me, "I learned right away that you had quite a reputation—Don't piss him off!—and that you were one of those guys who's totally unpredictable. Completely fuckin' inconsistent. A raving lunatic. A drunkard!"

He didn't waste any time asking Alex for a shift transfer.

"What's the problem?" Alex asked.

"No problem. I just prefer to work another shift."

"No. You're going to have to learn to work with everyone." Alex knew that if Eric got his way, the other guys in the detachment would try the same thing.

So Eric came up to me. "Billy, you and I have to have a chitchat."

I stood there, waiting.

"Let me tell you something. I've known alcoholics in my life, and you're one of them. I can tell by the inconsistency in your work habits. You never do the same thing twice. One day you're a friend, the next day you're an enemy. Well, I've got no use for an alcoholic."

I was stunned. No one had ever called me an alcoholic before. I had always thought alcoholics were brown-paper-bag bums, not men who get up every day and work for a living. His words sunk into me like a knife.

It was about a year before Eric and I became friends. Much later he told me his first impression: I was an incompetent sergeant by RCMP standards. "You didn't get my respect just from being a sergeant," he said. "But you never phoned in sick for ten consecutive years. That earned respect."

It seemed that the closer I came to cracking the organized theft rings, I was that much further away from being able to do anything about it. The web of corruption and deceit was way beyond me. People who seemingly had nothing to do with each other on the waterfront, were actually covering each other's butt. It was like a hall of mirrors, each mirror reflecting something that had never been seen before. And what made matters worse was I had no back-up. Denny had been promoted, so I was on my own. I was beginning to ask myself whether I should keep on going.

1O. FAMILY CRISES

When my eighteen-year-old son Steven started working on the waterfront, I knew he'd have a hard time because all the people who hated me—the long-shoremen, cops, and shipping agents—would take revenge on him. The cops who wanted to bust him would keep an eye out every time he got behind the steering wheel, and the others would try to get him fired any way they could.

The longshoremen and cops treated Steven as if he were my informant. They figured that if they gave him a hard time, I would back off. They soon realized they were messing with a shooter. I never acted on any information that was passed on to Steven; instead, I turned up the heat on the people I was going after. As they say in the wrestling business, "a shooter never backs down."

It was the summer of 1979. My sixteen-year-old nephew, Henry, was staying with Carol and me, and we'd noticed he was acting a bit strange. Normally talkative, he was withdrawn and sullen, and he didn't want to share his problems with us.

When he came home one evening, I told him, "You're going to go see Dr. Hayes. I made an appointment for seven o'clock this evening. And if you don't go, the cops, Dr. Hayes, myself, and your mother are going to have you committed."

He went.

After meeting with Henry, Kemp knew there was something wrong, but he didn't have enough information to get to the bottom of it. We didn't find out what was going on until two years later, when Henry's sister told us that his son, Jimmy, was being abused. When I pressed her, she said that's all she knew.

From the moment Henry introduced me to his girlfriend, Robin, I was put off by her. She was 5' 2" and heavyset. She dressed sloppily, as if she never considered that the colours of her clothes might clash. When we met, Robin seemed like a cheerful teenager, but my gut told me that she was not a good match for Henry. They got together when they were sixteen. Soon after that, she became pregnant.

The two of them split up when Jimmy was two. Not long after, Robin became involved with another young man, and had another child. At the time of Henry's current difficulties she was living with Jimmy, still two, and his younger brother, Tom, who was eight months old, in a two-bedroom apartment in Beaver Bank Villa fifteen miles from our home. Henry and Robin had been separated for about a year.

The thought of Jimmy being abused made my blood boil. I had never conducted this kind of investigation so it took me a little while to formulate a plan. A police friend of mine had a sister who was working at Children's Aid Society. I figured through her, we could initiate a timely intervention. I also wanted to see to it that our file received personal attention, rather than end up in a pile on someone's desk.

I phoned George, an RCMP friend who was living in Sackville, and told him what was happening. Without missing a beat, he said, "Let's go right now." When I told Henry what was about to happen, he was disoriented. He didn't even know what day it was. But he did as I asked and climbed into the car to ride with George to Robin's apartment at Beaver Bank Villa—an Army barracks that had been converted to living quarters after the Second World War.

Robin answered George's knock, and blocked their entry. "The kids are sleeping," she said. "I've already put them to bed." But Henry could hear the baby crying so he forced his way inside. Jimmy was standing in the smaller bedroom, looking dazed, with two black eyes and a six-inch bruise behind his left ear. One of the cuts on his back was still bleeding. Judging from the welts on his back, it looked like he had been beaten with a rope or an electrical cord. As Henry approached his son he saw cuts on his back and legs.

"He was beaten by a babysitter," Robin said.

Henry was in shock. All he could do was look from Robin to Jimmy, and back to Robin again. George went inside and called Children's Aid who came to the apartment within minutes. After photographing the children, he took them to the emergency room at the Children's Hospital.

That evening, Henry sat down in the front room. His expression was very sad. "Children's Aid is placing the children in a foster home," he said hollowly.

"That's the best goddamn thing that could happen!" I replied. I knew that neither Henry nor Robin was capable of looking after the kids. I was happy to hear that foster parents would be looking after him, even if it meant I wouldn't be seeing him anymore.

Just as we were getting over the nightmare about Jimmy, Carol's sister, Judy, was diagnosed with leukemia. To save Judy, Carol decided to have a bone marrow transplant. After a hell of a stressful period, the operation proved successful, and both sisters fully recovered. At forty-four, Carol was the oldest person and the first grandmother in the world to become a bone marrow donor[8]. Judy lived another twenty years.

It took Jimmy several months to recuperate in the hospital. When he was released, Children's Aid Society placed him in a foster home in Shelburne, about 120 kilometres from Sackville. His mother had returned to her home in Shelburne, and so it seemed odd that Jimmy was placed there. Henry had visiting rights but most times when he would show up, Jimmy wouldn't be there, so he ended up in loud verbal confrontations with Robin's parents and with others in the neighbourhood. Henry's anger and frustration at not being able to see his son was rising to the boiling point. Carol and I decided that we would try to gain custody, so retained my lawyer, Victor Goldberg.

Although I didn't attend the court proceedings in Shelburne, I understood that Victor presented an excellent case. A month later, Victor, Carol, Henry, and our daughter-in-law, Debbie (Scott's wife), drove to the court in Shelburne to hear the judge's decision. But Judge Comeau had been removed from the bench for health reasons, and they couldn't find his decision. We had to start all over again—this time in Yarmouth court, which tacked on another 110 kilometres to the drive. We were confident about winning so we packed a suitcase of clothing so that we could take Jimmy home with us.

Victor was going to be interviewing Jimmy during the court proceedings but Jimmy was nowhere to be found. The foster parents said they didn't know where he was. So a three-year-old boy just vanishes into thin air? I used every police source I could think of to try to locate Jimmy in Nova Scotia. I even went to three of my informants and offered them a $10,000 reward for locating the boy, and told my police friends there would be $10,000 for anyone who could find him. (Since it was illegal for them to claim it, they would have had a friend collect the reward for them.)

Everyone struck out.

Ten thousand dollars was a lot of dough back then, but still, no takers. That meant the chances of anyone finding Jimmy were slim. A thought had crossed my mind, and I confided in Eric.

"Since there has been no response, do you think someone might have taken Jimmy into the backwoods and done away with him?" I asked. "Maybe he's lying in an unmarked grave somewhere."

---

8 On March 7th, 1986 Carol received the International Women's Day award for Best Non-Fiction Story for an article she wrote about her bone-marrow transplant experience.

At first, Eric didn't answer. He just stared at me. Finally, he nodded his head, yes, got up and walked out.

Henry had told Jimmy what a tough cop and wrestler Billy Taylor was. I could just picture Jimmy wondering, "OK. So where is he now that I need him?" It was tearing my guts apart.

I knew that I might have to take some drastic action myself.

About two months later I received an urgent phone call from Victor. Children's Aid Society in Abbotsford, British Columbia had phoned.

Two years had passed since Jimmy had gone missing, and the Abbotsford police had found him!

Now five years old, Jimmy had been staying at a house in Abbotsford. An elderly lady who lived next door would bring him milk and cookies in the afternoon while he played in the yard. Because of the way he behaved—he was withdrawn and afraid to engage in conversation—she thought there was something wrong with him.

One day when Jimmy didn't show up to play, the lady called the police. When they questioned her, she said she didn't know who he was or who his parents were; she didn't even know his name. The two cops knocked on the door of the house where Jimmy had been staying, and a twenty-year-old girl answered. She claimed she had been looking after the house and assumed that the owners had taken the boy with them.

The cops invited themselves in to have a look around (without a search warrant). One of them opened the door to the front hall closet. He saw a large suitcase on the floor and kicked it to see if it was packed, thinking the young woman may have been about to leave. He heard a feeble cry and sprang open the latches. For the first half-second, he didn't recognize what was inside. Then he realized it was a young boy lying in a fetal position, gasping for breath and moaning. His back and arms were covered with bruises.

The cop looked up at the young woman, who seemed surprised to see Jimmy.

An ambulance rushed him to the emergency room of the nearest hospital. This time, it took Jimmy six months to recover.

The cops didn't get to first base with their investigation and the person or persons responsible for beating Jimmy were never brought to justice. I do know that Robin and her family had been anxious over the custody battle in Nova Scotia. I believe a family member took Jimmy to British Columbia, with the best of intentions, to ensure that their family would be able to continue to see the boy. What happened then, God only knows—or so I thought at the time.

Some twenty years later, out of the blue, Jimmy told me some of what he remembered. He doesn't know if he was left with a relative or a friend, but he remembers being mistreated by whomever was looking after him.

He recalled being forced to eat everything on his dinner plate whether he liked it or not. He wasn't allowed to speak in the house, and after supper, he was taken to his room and was not allowed out all night, even to go to the bathroom. He said it got worse, but so far he has not wanted to share any more with me.

Back when we started the custody battle for Jimmy, Victor and I filed a court order prohibiting anyone from removing the boy from Nova Scotia. That well-intentioned plan was backfiring on us. Now, only the person who abducted Jimmy could legally bring him back home, and of course that person would not come forward for fear of being charged.

Meanwhile, Children's Aid was not interested in footing the bill for a round-trip ticket to fly someone out to British Columbia to accompany Jimmy on a flight back to Nova Scotia. When I offered to pay, Children's Aid still declined. The court order in Nova Scotia would take precedence over any court order in another province, so we were stuck.

Children's Aid of British Columbia made the next move. They said that they weren't going to send him back to his home environment in Nova Scotia; they were going to put him in foster care. The nurse who had been taking care of Jimmy in the hospital wanted to adopt him. I felt strongly that such an adoption might work out in the short term, but that Jimmy would have no protection if she were to be killed in an accident. No one would know his whereabouts. I insisted that Jimmy stay connected to the family.

Victor contacted the best family lawyer in British Columbia, who told me there was little chance of returning the boy to Nova Scotia.

"If I take this to court," he told me, "I won't be able to win the case. The judge will say, 'We have to do what's in the best interests of the boy. He can make his own decisions when he turns sixteen.'"

"I tell you what. You take it to court, and you try."

"The expense is going to be astronomical. Just to take it to court is going to cost you a $5,000 retainer up front."

"I'll wire you the money so you'll have it tomorrow," I said. "Start legal proceedings NOW."

About a month later Victor told me that it wasn't going well in British Columbia. He didn't hold out much hope that the court would rule in our favour. Not the type to take 'No' for an answer, I devised an alternate plan. I contacted a private investigator friend who specialized in snatching children from cults and offbeat religious groups. He had just snatched a twelve-year-old girl in Antigonish and taken her home to her father in Texas. I would pay him and his female partner $5,000 to go to British Columbia, pretend to be Jimmy's parents, kidnap him, and bring him to New Brunswick where a friend and his wife would look after him until we could arrange to bring him home.

I was going to go to British Columbia to divert the cops, arriving three days early to familiarize myself with the lay of the land. I knew who the nurse was and where she lived. On the day of the planned kidnapping, I would go to downtown Abbotsford and set fire to a vacant building to tie up the local police. While the building was burning, I'd play the part of a mental case and run into a nearby business establishment, waving a gun and taking hostages to tie up additional police power. I figured this would give the snatchers at least a fifty-fifty chance of escaping. I would give up only if events caused me to endanger someone's life. To establish an alibi, I phoned a relative in Pasadena, California and told him that I might be dropping by for a visit at that time. Carol, who knew the plan, was going to fly to Bangor, Maine as a diversion.

On the morning of the day I was going to fly to British Columbia, Carol and I were sitting at the kitchen table having coffee. My suitcase stood by the door. Neither of us said a word for the longest time. I was thinking, 'Will I ever see Carol again?' We both knew that I would end up in jail, probably for several years. Carol was already planning to sell the house and move to British Columbia so she could visit me in jail. There was nothing for either of us to say. The silence hung in the air like a thick rain cloud. I wasn't even planning to say good-bye. In just a few minutes, I'd walk over, pick up my suitcase, and head out the door.

RRRIIINGG! The telephone jolted us.

"It was too late to call you last night," Victor began in an upbeat voice. "I heard from our man in British Columbia and because of the time difference, I figured I'd call you this morning instead."

"So what's the news?" I asked impatiently.

"Our man won the case! Jimmy is coming home!"

I put down the phone and let out a deep sigh.

Carol walked over to me, grabbed hold of my arms, and cried, looking into my eyes. After a moment I glanced out the front room window at the kids playing on the lawn across the street. It was a strangely quiet moment. I said to myself, 'Maybe there's a chance there's a God after all!'

Now that we knew Jimmy was coming home, we redoubled our efforts to adopt him. I met with Victor in his office. "Billy," he said, "I'm turning the case over to a new lawyer in our firm. I will remain involved but I believe that John Stewart is the man we need right now."

Changing horses in midstream did not appeal to me, but the more we talked, the more it made sense. I knew that investigators often run out of ideas and end up facing a brick wall. Maybe it was time for some new ideas.

From the moment Stewart and I shook hands, I was impressed. 'This guy is one sharp cookie,' I told myself. 'If John were a wrestler I'd chalk him up as a shooter.' His first move was to file papers to have the custody hearing held in Halifax.

Then he dropped the bomb. "I know you and Carol are responsible people to raise Jimmy but we have to demonstrate that to the court. I want you and Carol to undergo psychological testing. Doctor Hayes should be able to set up an appointment for you."

After I scraped my jaw off the floor I went through the motions of ending the conversation, and headed to Kemp's office.

I sure as hell didn't want to go through *that* again!

Kemp thought it was an excellent idea. "You not only need the best," he advised. "You need the one who will be the best in court. The one person who can do that is Ron Backman."

I hit the ceiling. Backman was the last person I wanted to see! He's the one I tried to prove was wrong about the physchologial testing.

Kemp glared at me. Finally, he said, "Are you thinking of yourself or the boy?"

I had a million excuses why things had gone wrong in my life, and Backman was one of them. But this time, I'd have to put myself aside. "OK. Make the appointment," I said. "I'll see Backman."

I entered his office with a sense of dread. "Hello. Remember me? Billy Taylor. Harbour Police." He nodded his head and motioned me to sit down.

"Why me?" was how he started the conversation.

"Because the experts tell me you're the best in the business," I said, swallowing my pride, "and with you on my team, we can win."

After discussing my case for the better part of an hour, Backman leaned toward me and said, "OK, Billy. I'll start working on it and I'll get back to you." He interviewed Carol and me at home, and our children at their homes. This time the court case was in nearby Dartmouth.

I was the first witness to give evidence for our side. Because of my training I just answered either 'Yes' or 'No'. The female Legal Aid lawyer asked me why I hadn't taken photos of Jimmy since I was a trained police Ident. officer.

"Had I taken the photos," I replied, "since I'm related to Jimmy, you would have objected to tendering them as evidence on the grounds that photos taken by a family member are highly prejudicial."

"I agree with Mr. Taylor," said Judge Paul Niedermayer.

That was one point for our team!

Dressed in a dark business suit, white shirt and tie, Backman sat in the witness stand for almost an hour. His soft-spoken and self-assured voice captivated everyone in the room, including the Judge, as if he had cast a spell. At that point, I felt overly confident we would win.

Finally, it was Carol's turn—her first time on the stand. She was doing fine until the end when her voice rose to a shrill pitch. I had been around courtrooms long enough to know what that meant. I closed my eyes and hoped the Judge would stop her, but he didn't.

Carol was almost shouting now: "Your Honour, we have done everything according to the law for the past two years and it seems like everyone is against us! My husband Billy who is a good husband and father, and a good policeman, was going to British Columbia to kidnap the boy! He was ready to give up a twenty-five-year career and go to jail all because no one would listen to us. What do we have to do for justice to prevail?"

A silence fell over the courtroom. The Judge ordered a twenty-minute recess. I met Carol out in the hallway. "I'm sorry, Billy," she said in a troubled voice. "I know I shouldn't have said that."

"Honey, you did just fine," I replied as I looked over her shoulder to see if anyone was coming to arrest me. I said to myself, 'We stand a snowball's chance in hell of winning this case.'

Back in court Judge Niedermayer said (paraphrasing): "The Taylors gave some very damaging evidence here today. Henry admitted that he told certain persons in Shelburne that if he could not visit Jimmy, he would burn down their home. Carol Taylor stated that her husband Billy had planned to kidnap the boy in British Columbia. This evidence showed that the Taylors were telling the truth. And that is what this hearing is about: telling the truth so a decision can be made. On the other hand, the mother here today never took the stand to testify. This also tells me something about the truth.

"I am awarding six months' temporary custody to the Taylors. This temporary custody will be overseen by Children's Aid Society who in turn will report to Mr. Backman, who in turn will report to the court. This case is closed."

Following the temporary custody period we were granted full custody. The case of Jimmy's kidnapping finally came to a close. His torturer remains at large today.

In April 2003, when Jimmy was in his twenties, he phoned me from Ontario where he lives with his wife and three-year-old son Henry, named after his granddad.

"I never told you everything that happened to me in Abbotsford," he said, "but I haven't forgotten."

11. IT'S OVER

Our court victory was a tremendous shot in the arm. It was as though the blood had drained out of my body, and now I was coming back to life. I have always worked hard to win—both in the ring and when I was chasing criminals. I suppose it's my way of getting back at bullies who made fun of me when I was a kid. We celebrated our victory in the typical Taylor fashion. We had a handful of friends over for a barbecue and I sucked back the rye until five o'clock the next morning.

Back on the waterfront, I ran into a relative at the Pier 28 Canteen. Bob and I used to sit down for a coffee about once a week. This morning we were seated at one of the picnic tables in the eating area. It was a sunny day, and the bars on the windows cast shadows across our section of the 100-by-40-foot room.

At fifty-two, Bob[9] was a fine-looking man and had an air of importance. I envied his six-foot-tall height. The way he peered from behind his thick black-rimmed glasses gave the impression that his words were well considered. He never seemed to talk off the top of his head.

When my sister Joan first met Bob he was playing in a dance-hall band part-time, mostly in his hometown of Springhill. Even though he had never taken a single music lesson, he could pick up any musical instrument and play it perfectly.

9 Bob passed away on August 26, 1999

"So how're sales going this week, Bob?" I asked to make conversation. He sold auto parts to service stations, garages, the container terminal, and every one of the shipping companies that did business at the Port. Spark plugs, carburetors, points, wiring—you name it, Bob sold it.

"Well, Billy, I'm going to tell you something that's been going on that you may not know about," he started haltingly. After taking a gulp of his coffee he leaned in closer. "There are middlemen in just about every organization up and down this waterfront who are pulling an auto parts scam. The company pays full price, and then the guy in charge of the stores department turns around and sells the item for cash at half price or less, and pockets the money. There's room for kickbacks to the shipping foremen, the guys who distribute the stores for the Port, and the mechanics who do the repairs. You should catch these bastards and put them in jail."

"That doesn't surprise me, Bob," I replied. "But I can't do a damn thing without proof. The only way I could catch someone red handed is to get someone to make a buy but even then, the officials would bury it so fast we wouldn't have a case." Meanwhile, I was thinking to myself: 'So I pay $100 for a starter when I could probably pick one up for $10!' The Rat once told me I could have my car fixed on a regular basis. Anything I wanted—All I had to do was ask! But I knew that the minute I fell for the bait the word would be out that I could be bought, and that would be the end of what I could do on the waterfront. That's why everyone hated me. I never played their game.

"Give me an example of one of these phony transactions," I said.

"OK. Let's say I go to the container terminal and ask, "What do you need in the way of parts this month?" The buyer reads off a list: 400 brake shoes, 300 distributors, and so on. I supply the order and invoice them at full price. The container terminal pays the bill. Nothing wrong so far. Meanwhile, inside the company, some of those parts are being sold dirt cheap, but there's no paper trail because they're all cash transactions."

I knew what he was talking about because my son Steven was working for a shipping company at the time. The ship's agent would regularly give him $40,000 to $60,000 US in cash, which he would deliver to the ship's Captain. The Captain would then buy supplies for the coming voyage, and pay the men's wages. The waterfront was swimming in cash. There were tons of opportunities for kickbacks.

After talking to Bob I went back to my routine police work—dealing with accidents, assaults, and parking violations. Hearing about the auto parts scam from a reliable source made me even more frustrated. Here's another example of theft and graft—happening all around me—and I can't do a damn thing about it. It's like having mice in the walls of your house destroying the insulation, and there's no way to stop them!

Then Alex resigned.

His departure was as quiet as his arrival had been bold. What tipped us off was the announcement of the new Chief and Deputy Chief. I had never gotten along with either of them. I had known it was coming because a retired federal government employee could only stay in another federal government job for ten years. They had to move on if they wanted to keep their pension. Both Donald Cassidy (the Director General) and Alex had begun their jobs a decade ago.

The Chief had certainly left his mark on the department. In the process of cleaning up the ranks and getting down to business, Alex had dismissed and resigned nineteen cops. In their place was a new breed of cops who were better educated, trained, and equipped.

The new Deputy Chief had never made an arrest in his life, and that bothered me. In his former job as Desk Sergeant, he had been constantly on my case for turning in reports with improper spelling and punctuation. As a Mountie, he had read and corrected reports. He was a nitpicker in my weakest area—writing. He used to mark up my reports in red ink and put notations in the margins, like a bloody school teacher.

We both started at the National Harbours Board together and were promoted at the same time—to Desk Sergeant and Sergeant. This was back when I arrested Buddy over the theft of canned frozen lobsters at the cold storage plant. There was no difference in pay or rank, but somehow he had the idea he was my boss from that point on.

Now that he was Deputy, he was the Big Cheese. He wanted us to search for stolen cargo in the stevedores' lunchroom lockers so he masterminded a raid at the container pier. They used to put booze in the lockers and leave them unlocked. That way, they could always say that someone else had put it there. (If they had used a lock, they would have incriminated themselves since only they had the key.) It made sense to move in on them for the booze, but not the way the Deputy had planned it. Our only hope for success was to catch them off-guard. That meant showing up in plainclothes in our own private cars. Even then there was no guarantee because I suspected there was a mole in the department—an ex-longshoreman who was working in the Criminal Investigation branch. As soon as he found out, he'd notify the men and blow our cover.

"Sergeant Taylor," he ordered, "you are to enter the container pier with eight men in uniform, in marked police cars."

"Sir, the minute they see us through the gate, they'll know it's a raid," I replied. "As a matter of fact, why don't I have the Stadacona band parade us in, or maybe we should send them a telegram ahead of time?"

I enjoyed being a wise ass, even if it did land me in hot water.

I went ahead with my original plan, which was to go in unmarked cars, wearing coveralls. The longshoremen greeted us with open arms saying, "We're some goddamned glad to see we've got police protection around here!"

I was ninety-eight per cent sure I knew who the informant was but with two per cent uncertainty, I couldn't risk it. Someone high up would cover his ass. It was like nailing an unfaithful spouse: you'd better be damned sure before you blow the whistle.

To be fair, the Deputy had a good reason to watch me like a hawk. My unpredictability made him edgy, just like it had the wrestlers. I did things my way and sometimes that meant breaking the rules, to get the job done. The Chief and Deputy seldom complained about my results, but sometimes they had a problem with my methods.

I can't remember the Deputy Chief ever saying a positive word to me. He was always looking for something to criticize. What really ticked me off is he never recognized my men for their accomplishments.

Not only was Eric Mott extremely capable, he would put his own life in jeopardy if it meant saving someone's life. One time, a Japanese seaman ran into trouble while cleaning a fish meal machine. He had opened the hatch of the fish grinder without purging the system and was overtaken by the ammonia fumes. By the time Eric got there, he had passed out, half inside and half outside the machine. I was stationed at the dispatch office desk, and immediately contacted the Halifax Fire Department Rescue Squad.

Moments later, I heard Eric's urgent voice on my radio: "Sarge, I have to crawl inside the machine to stop the blades from slipping or this guy is going to be fish meal." The only tool he could find to hold the blades in place was a five-foot long two-by-four. He grabbed it and climbed in.

A short time later I heard Eric's partner's voice on the radio: "Sarge, Eric is passing out," he said in a panic. "The blades are slipping. He'll be cut in two! Where's the fucking rescue squad?"

"They just passed the station," I said. "You should be able to hear the sirens now. Tell Eric to hold on for another thirty seconds."

The radio fell silent. I sat there with my head in my hands, expecting the worst.

Finally, Eric's partner's voice blurted out: "Sarge, the firemen stopped the blades from slipping. They used a heavy house jack. The ambulance is bringing Eric and the Japanese guy to the hospital."

Both of them fully recovered.

The next day, I submitted for a written commendation to recognize Eric's bravery. Instead, our Deputy said Eric had been completely out of line. He *reprimanded* him for attempting the rescue without a Scott-pack breathing apparatus!

"Sir, for your information," I politely informed the Deputy, "we don't have fucking Scott packs!" He thought we were equipped with these things but I had never seen one in all my years on the force. It turns out there were some stored at the Grain Elevator—the only place they had ever been used.

When Eric heard the Deputy's response, he threw himself back in his chair. "He wanted me to take an oxygen pack down there?" he said, exasperated. "I don't believe this! He must not know that ammonia is volatile, and that oxygen makes it explode!"

Not long after that, Eric saved the life of a twenty-year-old man. At the Halifax Police Department's request, we had dispatched our police boat directly underneath the Halifax side of the Macdonald Bridge, and aimed our spotlight to locate a jumper. Ron Ryan, the boat operator, radioed the jumper's location to Eric.

The jumper had climbed over the railing and was standing on a side ladder on the underside of the bridge. Eric had reached a point on the catwalk about ten feet below the jumper, when the fellow let go of the ladder. Eric caught him on the way down. He pulled him back in over the railing, pinned him, brought him up to the surface of the bridge, and turned him over to the city police.

In Ottawa, they've decorated guys for less than that.

The Halifax Police Chief commended his officers who assisted with the rescue, but once again, Eric was reprimanded! This time it was for not wearing a safety harness. In fact, the Port Police had never owned a safety harness, nor trained its members in how to use one. Four days later, the reprimand was upgraded from verbal to written. Eric was told his life insurance policy would have been revoked, had he died during the incident.

Management's action surprised many of the members, but not Eric. He knew he was not one of the chosen few, mainly because of his union position as Grievance Chairman. He was well known for not backing down from issues of fairness, and, on many occasions, had gone head-to-head with management to represent the interests of the members.

Another time, Kent Roulston should have been commended. There was a fire in the dust tank at the grain elevator. The firemen wouldn't douse it because if air had gotten into the dust system before the water, there would have been an explosion. I called in the Halifax Police Department.

Like gasoline or gunpowder, grain dust is extremely explosive when it comes into contact with fire. Before opening the dust system, the firemen wanted to take the precautionary measure of evacuating the homes within a five-block radius of the grain elevator. But it was two o'clock in the morning, so we decided against it. Despite the risk, we figured we'd douse the fire. A fireman, a Halifax Police member, one of my members, and I would open the system and place a fire hose inside—and that would be that.

That's when Kent walked in. He opened up the dust system, shoved the water hose in, and doused the fire. Later, the Chief reprimanded him, saying that police have no business fighting fires.

Myself with Constables Kent Roulston
(left) and Eric Mott (right), 1989.
Photographer unknown.

In another incident, a fifty-year-old male patient walked out of the Halifax Infirmary on Queen Street, proceeded east on Morris Street to Cunard's Wharf, jumped into the harbour and drowned. Even though the Halifax Police and Ports Canada carried out investigations, neither got to the heart of the matter.

By working his connections at the hospital, Eric found out that the last person to talk to this man was a minister from Sackville, so he went and took a statement from him. As it turned out, the minister's remarks may have driven the man to kill himself.

The next day, the Deputy called Eric and me into his office and told us that we were "not to interfere with another department's investigation". That was a load of shit because anything that happened in the harbour was under our jurisdiction. The Deputy tore up Eric's report and statements and threw them in the waste can. Then he said, "If you continue to do things your own way without permission, you will be charged and reprimanded."

I must have submitted more than a dozen requests for the men to receive commendations from Ottawa for their acts of heroism, but they never got past the Deputy Chief's office. Maybe he was protecting his ass from being chewed out for not equipping the men with the proper safety gear.

Soon afterward I injured my lower back while installing a new bay window at home, and had to book off sick for a day. Since I was scheduled to appear as a witness for the prosecution in court, the department wasn't pleased—even though this was my first sick day in ten and a half years!

That afternoon, my neighbour phoned. "Billy," he said, "there's some guy outside my door. I think he's looking at your home through binoculars." With all the waterfront crooks to watch, the Chief was spying on me!

I made sure it was obvious that I was looking at him with my binoculars so he'd know his stakeout was burnt. A few minutes later he rang my doorbell. "I was just in the Sackville area on some business," he said, "and was concerned how you were feeling so I thought I would stop by to say hello. I hope you get well soon."

Just in case he thought I was a rookie investigator, later I checked the mileage for the car he used that day, and the times it was checked out and returned. The mileage was exactly from the station to my home and back. It was bad enough having the Deputy on my case while I was on duty, but now the Chief was checking up on me at home!

On a sunny spring day in 1984, my men and I were providing police security at a private showing of offshore oil equipment in Sheds 23, 33, and 34. The public was invited to attend in the afternoon, but in the morning it was an invitation-only event. I had stationed one uniformed officer and one plainclothesman in each shed. As the Shift Sergeant, I was letting my men handle the event while I patrolled the south end. Kent was stationed in plainclothes at the gate to make sure everyone who entered had a pass.

I heard Kent's voice on the radio: "I have a situation and I need a supervisor here, please."

As I was pulling into the lot I saw three guys in their twenties wearing jeans and sports shirts, trying to crash the gate.

"Lookit," said the most vocal one. "We're going in and you can't stop us."

"OK, OK. No reason to get excited, boys," I said, standing in front of them. They had obviously been drinking so I was trying to defuse the situation before it got ugly. "All you have to do is kill some time and come back at one o'clock when she's open to the public." They weren't buying it. I caught the look of determination in their eyes and called for back-up. "If you don't leave the premises," I added, "I'm going to place you under arrest for trespassing."

When they continued to whine ("You've got no authority to stop us, You're a bunch of pricks, You're a regular shit"), I warned, "When that car gets here, you can either walk away or we're going to drive you to the lock-up for trespassing." That must have convinced them because they turned around and headed north.

As they were walking away, the Chief radioed me to bring my entire shift back to the station. (He had been listening in on the police radio.) I left a man at Shed 23 and brought the others in. Three men flanked me on either side as we stood at attention in the Chief's plush red-carpeted office. The Deputy Chief was sitting next to the Chief. After I saluted the Chief, he got right to the point. "Sergeant Taylor," he said, "explain what just transpired in Shed 23."

"Sir, we had three young intoxicated men without passes who wanted to enter the oil equipment exhibition. They were refused entry."

"What were their names?"

"I never asked their names." I didn't know where his line of questioning was going and I was starting to feel boxed into a corner.

Growing impatient, the Chief asked in a more high-pitched voice: "Why didn't you ask their names?"

"Because they weren't under arrest."

"Well, why didn't you arrest them then?" he thundered.

"It didn't warrant an arrest." Much as I wanted to throttle this guy for second guessing me, I remained calm. "We just got rid of them. Had we attempted to arrest them, it would have probably caused a disturbance for the guests in Shed 23, and these people came to the Port of Halifax partly because of our high level of security and the way we handle things."

At this point the Chief sat back in his chair and crossed his arms on his chest. He looked at me with disgust and said, "Sergeant Taylor, do you know what your problem is?"

I didn't have a clue what he was talking about—since *he* was my problem. I stared at him blankly.

"Your problem, and the reason you didn't arrest them, is you're gutless."

I was looking straight into the Chief's eyes when he said this. My first thought was to unfasten my gun belt, walk over to his desk, and show him just how gutless I am. As I reached to unclasp the belt, I caught a glimpse of Eric's face. He was shaking his head, maybe half an inch, back and forth—just enough for me to see—and he was mouthing *No*. I took his advice and just stood there looking at the Chief until we were dismissed.

Had I followed my instincts, I would have played right into the Chief's hands. I would have pounded him right then and there and been fired for it, and quite possibly charged with assault. Eric's glance had saved me.

As soon as we were dismissed I got into my cruiser, drove to Shed 21, and took a seat in the lunchroom. A few minutes later a couple of the guys brought me a coffee.

"Fuck it. I quit," I told my buddies as I took a sip. They sat there silently and let me speak. "I'd rather pump gas or go drive a truck, than stay in this hellhole."

In one fell swoop, the Chief had cut me in two. I had a reputation as a shooter, as the guy not to fuck with. Whenever a tough situation came up, they called me. I had been the self-defense instructor for the police for twenty-two years, for God sakes, and he's calling me gutless? I sat there for the rest of the day and stewed, got into a forty-ouncer that night, and decided to start looking for a job over the next couple of weeks.

Gutless! I remembered one of the incidents I had been commended for during my police career. It took place at the corner of Sackville and Grafton Streets on October 11, 1969. A disturbed young man flailing a bayonet was threatening to kill a young mother and her baby. I disarmed him, threw him to the ground, and held him until the city cops arrived to arrest him. For this I received commendations from Halifax Police Chief George Robinson, Director General Cassidy, and Chief Alex Taylor.

And *I'm* gutless!

Our shift was the shining star in the Port Police. We filed fifty-seven per cent of all departmental reports, with only four out of eighteen members. We consistently had the lowest amount of sick time and the best court results.

Many years later, Eric told me, "When you think about it, what they did was they ended up putting all of the troublemakers in one shift. But that was their mistake because they actually ended up putting all the honest guys in one shift. They could never use one of us against the other."

"Kent, me, and you were three honest guys," he went on. "We were all pigheaded, set in our ways, very demanding, and assertive. We weren't in the chosen group. We were the honest group, and that meant we were the outcasts. We weren't getting promoted; we weren't going anywhere. If we had been in the chosen group, we would have been decorated twice, maybe three times."

The incident with the Chief took the stuffing out of my men. They figured if *I* was gutless, then what were *they*? Why bother even trying? Better to just sit there like a piece of shit on a log.

Ironically, just as I was about to start looking for work, Ottawa sent word down that I should attend a two-week course at the Transport Canada Training Institute in Cornwall, Ontario. I needed a change of pace and besides, the new Director General, Ted Ciunyk, would be there. I wanted to let him know about some of the bullshit that was going on in Halifax—or at least the thought had crossed my mind.

Sergeant Don Harvey and I went to Cornwall. The senior sergeants from all the Canadian ports whom we had met at previous courses were there.

Senior Police Supervisor Course, Cornwall, Ontario, 1984: Director General Ted Ciunyk, Ottawa (front row, third from left), myself (front row, far right) and Sergeant Don Harvey (back row, second from left). Photographer unknown.

Even though we didn't talk about it, they could tell something was wrong.

I didn't approach the Director General until October fourth—the second to last day of the course. I wanted to tell him how the members had been treated, but I was nervous.

Before the banquet I went up to him and asked if I we could talk for ten or fifteen minutes in confidence. "Yeah, sure," he said and led me into an office off the banquet room.

"Sir, I'm having a morale problem," I finally said after beating around the bush. "It's not only myself; it's all of my members. We've always done an excellent job. You can see the statistics. We out-produce the other three shifts combined. My men aren't afraid of work, but every time we do something good, we're put down for it." I paused to see if I should keep going. His deadpan expression didn't give me a clue. I was coming up with some serious information about my superior officers. 'Who's this lowly sergeant from Halifax to be telling me this, anyway?' is what I figured he was thinking.

"One of my men used up all of his compassionate leave days when his father died so he didn't have any left when it was time for the burial. He wasn't permitted to attend the funeral!

"I've put in for commendations for my men and never heard back. In fact, they were reprimanded for their acts of bravery. What we get is continual criticism from our officers. Recently, I was called in to explain the way I handled a situation, and I had handled this particular incident properly. Because I hadn't made an arrest I was called 'gutless' in front of my men."

"These are very serious accusations you've made against your superior officers," the Director General replied. "I hope for your sake Sergeant Harvey can corroborate this."

"I don't know, Sir. I can't speak for Sergeant Harvey. He'll have to speak for himself."

The Director General motioned for me to go get him. When we came back in, Don and I stood before him. The Director General said: "I dare say you know what Sergeant Taylor and I have been talking about. Would you corroborate what he has said?"

"I'm sure everything Sergeant Taylor told you was the truth," Don said without hesitation.

On hearing this, the Director General looked upset, as if to say, 'I'm sorry you told me this. You've ruined my day.' He cleared his throat and said, "OK. When you go back to your detachment, don't tell anyone about this conversation."

During the banquet I had butterflies in my stomach. Because of the DG's poker face, I had no idea how he might follow up on this. I felt like I was dangling on a string in the wind.

After the course finished up, I visited some relatives and friends in Ottawa before heading back to Halifax. I looked up John Sheir, a long-time friend who was a psychiatrist and a professor at Carleton University. One of his areas of specialization was the sleep patterns of shift workers. When we were catching up on old times at his home, I told him about some of the problems I had had in school as a kid. He gave me a test, right then and there. When he saw how I had filled it out, John said I was dyslexic.

Here I was, fifty-two years old, and it was the first time I had heard this!

"In your day," he explained, "you were just dumb, stupid, and rebellious. They didn't understand this at the time."

I wondered what difference it would have made if my teacher and parents had realized I was dyslexic and given me the help I needed, instead of calling me names and putting me down.

"You are one of the ones that's overcoming it, to a certain extent," John said, "but you never will completely."

I had been overcoming it all right—with booze.

Two weeks later, back in Halifax a notice was posted on the bulletin board in the Ports Canada Police station. Every member of our detachment was to attend a meeting at seven o'clock the following evening in the police lecture room. No exceptions.

There were shivers up and down my spine. I had an idea what the meeting was about, and I was afraid. My discussion with the DG had opened a can of worms, and now we were going to see how it was going to play out. I was afraid none of the other guys would back me up.

I arrived early in the 200-by-60-foot room and watched everyone filter in. All thirty-two members were there, plus the brass. Most of them were puzzled; they hadn't a clue why we were there. Only Don and I could guess.

Once the meeting was called to order, the DG addressed the department: "Good evening, gentlemen. Is there anybody here who has any complaints about this department?"

The Chief immediately spoke up. "Sir, I'm sure there's nobody here who has any complaints."

The DG whispered a few words in his direction, and carried on.

After about thirty seconds of silence, some of the men began to fidget.

Eric's hand went up.

Looking at the DG, he said: "My wife had just gotten out of hospital with a C-section and I put in for special leave. It was a very bad delivery and she needed personal attention at the house. He said, 'That's not a natural birth,' and wouldn't even give me my own vacation time!"

Next, I stood up.

"My members do an excellent job and they're reprimanded for it. Whatever I suggest, I'm criticized and put down. I'm told I don't know what I'm talking about. I've taken Criminal Investigation and Criminal Identification. I'm the only one in this department who's qualified in these fields, but it seems I don't know what I'm doing, or what I'm talking about. It doesn't make sense to have someone tell me about Investigation and Identification when they have never been trained in these areas themselves.

"I've heard some of the other members complain about how they're treated. There's a member who ran out of leave and requested one day's leave to attend his father's funeral. The leave was denied. Since our cheques are late getting here, another member asked for twenty minutes to go across the street to his bank. They made him sign a vacation leave form!" My voice was becoming shrill. I was starting to lose it, so I shut up and sat down.

The Director General asked, "Any other complaints?"

Albert stood up and said, "Sergeant Taylor forgot to tell you the Chief told Sergeant Taylor he was gutless."

The Director General said, "That's enough. Everybody is dismissed." The meeting had only lasted ten minutes.

I took an unmarked car to Halterm (the container terminal) and pulled it into the parking lot. I was thinking how fast the meeting went. They should have asked me more, I should have said more. More guys should have spoken up. There's going to be trouble over this.

"What's your 1020, Car Three?" came over the radio. ("1020" is police talk for "location".) I answered and a couple of minutes later two marked cruisers and five civilian cars pulled up.

One of the men hopped out of a civilian car, came over, and bent down to tell me the news. Both the Chief and Deputy Chief had just resigned.

I was just starting to think how nice it was going to be to have these guys off my case, when I realized that I would be paying for this big time. After all, I was the instigator for this meeting, and that doesn't go unnoticed among the top brass at Ports Canada administration. My reputation as a "troublemaker" was about to take on a new meaning.

A few days later, a shipping official named Jack Delaney came up to me while I was walking my beat. Jack was a wrestling fan. We used to bump into each other almost every day. "Sergeant Taylor, you've done some good things here, but you're walking a tightrope now," he said. "Someday someone's going to shake the rope and you're going to take a long, hard fall."

"I'll just open my parachute" was my smart-ass reply.

Jack threw me a serious look. "For your sake, Billy, I hope the chute opens before you hit the ground."

I've remembered Jack's words many times since.

My former partner, Denny, was promoted and that gave me pretty much free rein. But I still had to contend with the new Chief, Sid Peckford (Brian Peckford's[10] brother), who had been watching me like a hawk. Just about every

---

10 Brian Peckford was Premier of Newfoundland in the 1980s.

time I turned around it seemed like I was an inch away from being reprimanded or charged.

When Eric raided the stevedore locker room at Halterm and seized $10,000 worth of cargo liquor, both he and I were reprimanded for acting on our own. Another time, a freight handler was bothering waterfront workers about the hours they were working and other union matters, and it was interrupting their work. Longshoremen were not being paid good money to stand around and talk. Besides, the Ports Canada Bylaw 1-A states: "Only persons gainfully employed or who have legitimate business are permitted on port property." This person was neither, so I told him, "If you're not working here, leave, or we're going to charge you with trespassing."

"Oh yeah?" he replied. "I'll bring five or six of my buddies down here and we'll spread you all over these fuckin' railway tracks."

In the heat of the moment, I patted my sidearm and said, "Just try it and there will be six dead bodies all over the fucking railway tracks, not one dead cop." What I *should* have said was, "You're under arrest for threatening a police officer," or "for harassing a police officer in the line of duty."

Instead, I squared off. Looking directly at him, I placed my left thumb on my gun belt and my right hand on my gun holster. "Go get your buddies and try it," I said.

He told Chief Peckford that I had threatened him. That earned me another reprimand.

In the midst of all this, Chief Peckford said he wanted to send me on a five-week Senior Police Administration Course at the Canadian Police College in Ottawa. I figured it was because I was the department's most senior sergeant at the time. The purpose of this course was to train police sergeants in managerial skills so the members under our command can carry out their duties and responsibilities with as little stress as possible from the sergeant and the management. That made sense to me!

All of the senior police sergeants from the twenty-four major police forces in Canada would be there.

Participants at the seventh Senior Police Administration Course at the
Canadian Police College, Ottawa, 1986. I'm the short guy in the middle
row (left). Sergeant Joe Rogers from Fredericton is in the front row, far
left. Deputy Chief Terry Rouse ("The Dep") from Dieppe is in the middle
row, far right.
Photographer unknown.

Since I was on the outs with the new Chief, I figured maybe he was setting
me up for a fall. With my lack of education it would be tough to pass the course,
so I busted my butt studying.

Although I had a lot of fun with the other sergeants—especially the practical
jokers—I spent most of my time with the books. The final exam on Friday morning
was the most difficult exam any of us had ever written during our entire
police careers.

We all felt that we had passed, and so we were breathing easy by the time
the graduation luncheon rolled around. There was more brass at the head table
than I had ever seen at a police function.

The class president, RCMP Sergeant Joe Rogers of Fredericton, addressed
the assembly: "Although we wear different uniforms, we still have the same
goals at heart. A common objective, if you will. I can safely say that leadership
abounds among the members of SPAC 86-7. With men such as these in our
midst, I believe that the law enforcement of this country is in extremely capable
hands."

Joe's words made me feel proud for the first time in a long while.

Just before the meal was served, with some of the administrators, cooks,
and cleaning staff standing by, Joe said, "There is one more presentation to be
made at this time. There is a man among us who, in my mind, outshone us
all. His personality and temperament were such that he stole our hearts from
day one. To me, he is the epitome of honesty, truth, and honour. His rendition
of how he broke the principal's arm and threw him down the stairs that first

day broke the ice for all of us and set the mood for which we were to become noted during our time at the Canadian Police College. He was especially good to everyone but exceptionally so to three in particular, Terry "the Dep" (short for Deputy Chief), Barney, and myself. So, we decided that Billy should have something to remember us by. Billy, you're the kind of man that poets and songwriters write about. It is with great pleasure and deep respect that I present to you this plaque. I hope in some small way it will help you think of us all from time to time."

At that point, all of the senior police sergeants stood to applaud, along with the College staff. Looking back over my entire thirty-one-year police career, that was my finest hour.

The plaque I received at the SPAC course, 1986.

Photograph by Lysia Taylor.

Today, that plaque is on my office wall, and I will pass that letter on to my grandchildren, just as I would have liked my grandfather to have left me something to be proud of.

When I arrived home I was told that I had made the highest mark on the exam of any Ports Canada policeman to date!

Not long after that luncheon the department played its hand. The Chief wanted to know what kind of figures would look attractive to me in a pension offer. When we finally came to an agreement, I was told to meet with Chief Superintendent Beveridge on August 20th at two o'clock pm. I showed up at the police station on time to find out that the appointment had been cancelled.

Two weeks later I wrote to Ottawa about this failed appointment. That letter must have gone into the same black hole that had swallowed all of my previous letters to Ottawa.

So I put my pension plans aside and spent more time on Ident work in the police photo dark room and lab. I was starting to burn out.

One day Chief Peckford called me on the carpet because a civilian had laid a complaint against me for using obscene and insulting language with the public. I was surprised to hear about this incident because I never knew that a member of the public had been within earshot of the conversation in question. I had been talking to my buddy Harvey.

Not long before this, Harvey had found out that he was dying of cancer. I didn't want him to have to deal with any more stress so I told him I'd take the heat for this, figuring it would probably mean a day's suspension.

I was charged and paraded. The charge read: "Using obscene and insulting language towards a member of the public." Even my worst enemies—both police and waterfront workers—were saying I was being set up for a fall.

I pled not guilty at the hearing. My lawyer figured I would receive a letter of reprimand.

Even though he had proven my case beyond a reasonable doubt, I was found guilty and was demoted two ranks to constable!

It was all falling into place, with me at the bottom of the heap. This would mean a decrease in pay of approximately $5,000 a year, which would also decrease my pension. I had four years to go before retirement, so the total damage would be a $20,000 hit, plus possibly a $10,000 decrease in my pension.

They must have figured this would get rid of me. I had "too much information" about certain people in high positions, and this made them feel uncomfortable. On top of that, my unpredictability made them nervous.

Years later, I was talking to my good friend Eric Mott about this.

"When they can't buy guys or control them, they put them in their crosshairs," he said. "The ones who were dishonest hated you. They couldn't steal anything when you were around. They'd rather have people who wouldn't say there's theft in the police department. They didn't want anyone rocking the boat."

I can remember a contract negotiation meeting where Chief Peckford said that in order to grant us the raise we wanted, he would have to lay off two members. So we had to choose between throwing two junior members out of work, or getting our raise.

I stood up and pointed out that it cost $1.25 million a year to run our department. I also cited an article in that day's paper saying that the Port of Halifax had made a record profit of $7 million that year. "So what's the big fucking deal in paying us what we want?" I asked.

My superiors didn't appreciate being put on the spot like that, in front of the men.

I had poured my life into my work for thirty years—for what? To be demoted, just when I should be going out in style and entering my golden years. The day I was notified about the demotion, I filed an appeal.

While I was waiting for a decision, I met with a few of my cop buddies at a Tim Hortons in Dartmouth. We were talking about my goddamned long, drawn-out court case. They were all looking at me funny, as if they knew something I didn't. Finally, my friend Harv Boutilier said, "What's all this doing to your family, Billy? What's it doing to your kids, and what's it doing to Carol?"

"Carol backs me up 100 per cent in this. She's ready to fight the bastards as long as it takes to get this straightened out."

Then I got the message. All of a sudden realized that fighting to reclaim my rank as sergeant was actually putting a tremendous strain on Carol and the kids, and my buddies could see it. I figured maybe it just ain't bloody worth it. It wasn't until five years later, when I was talking to a good friend of Carol's, that I found out just how stressed Carol had been at this time. She had been having crying spells at work—unknown to me and my alcoholic mind. She had been close to a nervous breakdown and had talked about admitting herself to a mental institution. Her big question was: could she stay married to me and keep her sanity? We had fallen in love the day we met, and then we fell more in love every day afterwards. The problem was, Carol would never leave me.

After two months of agonized waiting, the appeal court reached a decision: I would be reinstated to the rank of sergeant and they offered to make up my back pay from the day of my demotion, in return for my resignation with full honours.

I knew they couldn't do that and get away with it because the constables on the force would use it as a precedent to demand sergeant's pay for past time served. The smart ass in me wanted to use this as leverage to push them further and make them squirm, but I didn't have any fight left in me. Knowing I couldn't put Carol through any more, I took the offer.

I had finally shot with the shooters on the big mat—and lost.

Not long after, Lloyd Osborne, a friend and union rep, phoned to invite me to come down to the station so the department could give me a retirement gift. I said to myself, 'Big fucking deal!' Then, I figured, what the hell? I'll go just to humour them. Carol was so mad about how I had been treated that she stayed home. Lloyd had been downplaying the event just to get me to show up.

When I walked into the police boardroom, it was a full-blown going-away party! There were cops from every department along with retired cops I had worked with over the years, including Clary Bayers, the first port cop who broke me in to the ways of the waterfront. Joe Ross, Executive Director of the Police Association of Nova Scotia, was there along with a number of PANS members. Ports Canada's civilian staff from every department was there. There were also freight handlers, stevedores, and checkers—including some I had charged over the years.

I was shocked to see such a turnout!

Deputy Director General Beveridge from Ottawa was there, as was Alex Taylor (it was his first time at the station since he retired). Seeing Alex meant a lot to me.

Former Chief Alex Taylor (left) and myself at my retirement party, 1989.
Photographer unknown.
Retirement plaque, 1989. Photograph by Lysia Taylor.

I felt proud. As I blew out the thirty-one candles on the anniversary cake I was thinking, 'Now, this whole thing isn't ending half bad!'

Port Manager David Bellefontaine presented me with a beautiful wall photo of the Port of Halifax, and I left with enough gifts to fill the back seat of my car.

As I walked out of the station, I thought about the complex web of crime on the waterfront and the corruption that was going on beneath the surface of what most people knew.

I thought about the manager who was being paid $750 every month for car expense, even though he didn't own a car, and he didn't drive.

Goods were being re-routed every day. There were individuals at the Port, both inside and outside Ports Canada Police, who were afraid that once somebody tumbles, that could set off a domino effect that would expose everyone.

They had good reason to be nervous.

Their solution was to get rid of the troublemakers. Four other cops who saw the writing on the wall left in 1989 and 1990. The average Haligonian didn't have a clue what was really going on down here. There was no way of knowing how much crime we had prevented these past twenty-one years since Don Cassidy and Alex Taylor began the fight in 1968.

I recalled when my partner, Albert Gagnon, and I first met up with organized crime members in the late 1960s. We arrested two black-leather-jacketed men on motorcycles who had previously been charged with rape. We were sure they had stolen cargo because they had been hanging around the sheds when there were no ships in port. But since we didn't have proof, all we could charge them with was speeding under the Government Property Traffic Act. As it turned out, they were members of the Thirteenth Tribe, the organization that later became the Hell's Angels.

I recalled in 1971, investigating the theft of a shipment of weapons from Shed 34. Later I found out that the crooks were organized crime members. I held one of them in custody but had to release him because I didn't have enough proof. Of course, in the wrestling business I had rubbed shoulders with quite a few organized crime members. That was where I learned they're not confined to one level of society. They're just as happy to do business with top-level administrators and middle management, as with low-lifes.

The theft that was going on that involved port workers and organized waterfront crime was way more than anyone could keep track of, much less get a handle on, and God knows, I'd tried!

They must have breathed easy as I walked out that door.

12. THE RUG IS PULLED OUT FROM UNDER ME

For the first two months of my "retirement" I couldn't take any other work because I had to finish my thirty-one years before I was eligible for my pension. So I turned into a homebody—lounging around in my favourite easy chair, wearing slippers, smoking my pipe, and playing with Shamus, our Golden Lab. I got to spend a lot of quality time with Shamus while my cat, Cuddles, looked at me as if to say, "What in the hell are *you* doing here?" (Or was she jealous?)

It was the life. No more pulling all-nighters, chasing crooks between boxcars and sheds, and taking crap off every sonofabitch I met. Now that we had time to think about the future, Carol and I planned to buy a travel trailer the following year when she retired and visit the vacation spots we had missed on our trips to Florida. Carol and Billy Taylor were two fortunate people: the world was our oyster.

I had told Roger Miller, the Maritimes District Manager for Pinkerton's of Canada, that I would be available to start work as a security guard on January eighth.

Roger Miller, former Maritime District Manager, Pinkerton's of Canada.
Roger is currently Vice President, Operations, Northeastern
Investigations Inc. Courtesy Northeastern Investigations, Inc.

At six o'clock that evening, the phone rang. "If you're finished sitting on your lazy ass, do you want to go to work tonight?" Roger asked. I started two hours later.

In his early thirties, Roger was a good-looking man and an exceptional dresser. He usually wore a dark business suit, white shirt, dark tie, and black shoes that would make a Marine drill sergeant smile. There was never one hair out of place on his head, which always made me want to muss it up!

When I first met Roger I could tell he was a bloody Pinkerton's detective. His slim 190-pound frame was ramrod straight whether he was standing or walking. He'd be all over you like an octopus in a confrontation.

Although most of my time had been spent chasing thieves, my work as a Criminal Identification Officer—both at the Port and with the Halifax Police Ident Section—had given me a broader range of experience. Because of my involvement with other crimes including arson, robbery with violence, sexual assault, willful property damage, and fatal industrial accidents I was a valuable candidate for Pinkerton's.

As a cop I used to walk a beat and keep my eye on an entire sub-community. Now I had to sit at a desk and screen the people as they came in, or watch over a high-security area such as an art gallery or bank vault. On the more active assignments, I got to stretch my legs, roving inside and outside the building to keep an eye on the entries and exits.

I figured I'd get farthest in this line of work by looking and acting like a dumb security guard. The client, whether it was Dalhousie University, the Bank of Montreal, or Acadian Lines, didn't need to know I had been a top criminal investigator with the Port Police, and no one needed to know about my stint as a self-defence instructor or my wrestling background. That way, people would open up to me. Clients would tell me about items, money, or booze that had gone missing, and I knew they were probably the culprits. They would often hire security to "protect" themselves from their own inside job. The Pinkerton's guard would provide these crooks with an extra layer of protection in a way that wasn't obvious.

Thinking back on my security details, there were at least twenty-five incidents where managers or supervisors had stolen from their own companies, and then blamed the "dumb security guard" for allowing someone to walk off with the loot. If I ever confronted the guilty party, I'd get the boot.

When I saw security guards dipping into the till, I'd say, "You're no different from the fucking thieving cops I used to work with." I was fighting the system, just like I did on the waterfront.

One evening a conversation with Carol quickly turned to a problem she was facing at the car dealership where she worked. One of her duties was to count the money at the end of the day and lock it in the safe. She and the president of the company had the only keys. The next morning the cashiers would come up short.

Carol always put a rubber band around each bundle of bills, and slipped a piece of paper under the elastic showing the count. I advised her to double count the bills in each pile before putting them in the safe, and then count them the next morning before handing them to the cashiers. One bill was missing from each pile. I was sure it was the president of the dealership. He could easily come in at night when everyone was gone, lift a bill off each pile, and make it look like Carol was to blame.

"Tomorrow, when you count the bills," I advised her, "have someone you trust witness the count and initial the bundles. The next day, when you go to open the safe, call in the boss so he can see you unlock it. Next, count the bundle of bills, and pass them to the cashier."

One bill was still missing from each bundle, for a total of $100 a day. "It appears we have a major theft problem here," Carol told her boss. "Do you want me to report this to the city police?"

"No, Mrs. Taylor," he said evenly. "That won't be necessary."

Talking about it that evening over a drink, we both felt this was very odd. Not report it! If it were my company, I'd call in Scotland Yard to catch the sonofabitch who was robbing me blind.

As it turned out, it was not the boss. Soon after Carol left the company, I found out that the boss's daughter had been going out with a con artist and thief. The president must have solved this himself. If he had called the cops, they would have dragged his daughter through the mud.

If crooks knew I was an experienced investigator, they would watch every word they said to me. I've always preferred they underestimate my intelligence and show their cards—just like on the waterfront and in the wrestling business. In Roman Greco matches, I would start off pleading with my opponent: "I don't know too much about this. Promise you won't hurt me." Then I'd let him throw me down on the mat. Sooner or later, he'd get careless and when I saw an opening I'd start to shoot. He'd swear to God someone had a fucking vise on him!

This sort of unpredictability got me kicked out of wrestling, but in the security business it was an asset.

My first assignment was at the Bank of Montreal's Main Branch on George Street in downtown Halifax. They were doing repairs that required shutting down the alarm system, and I was supposed to keep an eye on the main vault. After that I was stationed on the fourth floor in the cheque-separating department where Pinkerton's provided twenty-four-hour security. That's where I found out about a job servicing Bank of Montreal money-dispensing machines in Wolfville, in the Annapolis Valley.

The interviewer was the head of the bank's security for all of eastern Canada. As soon as I walked into his office and sat down I could tell he had been a Mountie. All that was missing was his red coat and spurs. He was a partially balding heavyset man in his sixties with a roundish face. When he spoke, I listened for the answer so I'd be prepared when he asked a question.

Right off the bat he started telling me my duties before I even had the job!

"Excuse me, Sir, for interrupting," I said, "but I thought this was an interview for the job. You're talking as if I'm already hired."

After a few strained moments of silence, he said with a flushed look on his face, clearly upset, "You *are* hired, Billy. I understand everyone calls you Billy, isn't that right?"

I could tell by the way he answered me—his body language, eye contact, whispering, and pronouncing every word as if he were God—that this guy was a former RCMP superintendent.

"Yes. That's correct, Sir," I managed as if responding to the superintendent back at the Police College.

"I know all about you from the day you were born," he continued, hands folded on the desk in front of him. He then looked down at his hands and paused as if he were praying, or searching for the correct words. Then he looked me in the eye and almost whispered: "Billy, I like to take a drink myself. Watch your drinking while you are working for this bank."

"Sir, I promise there will be no bottles while I am working for this bank. I'll eat oranges and other kinds of fruit instead. It's much better for me anyway."

At that point he folded his arms on his chest and leaned back in his chair wearing a smile about a foot wide—just as Chief Alex Taylor had looked when I told him the same thing twenty-one years earlier.

After only two months, my job at the bank came to an abrupt halt. One day I was taking $140,000 from the vault to fill the bank machines at Acadia University and a shopping mall. A bank employee said to me, "Don't shoot!"

Without thinking I replied, "You don't have to worry about that. I don't carry a gun." Until then no one knew that I wasn't carrying a gun. Because of all the hell I had been through with the Port Police over guns and psychological testing, I had decided not to carry one. That slip blew my cover.

When I was a cop, they didn't want me to carry a gun. If I did, they would fire me. Here, I was fired for *not* carrying a gun.

At my next job, I was sworn in as a special constable with the Halifax City Police Traffic Division and served traffic summonses in Halifax County. I actually enjoyed showing up for work at the police station, not having to carry a gun. During this period I was drinking heavily. Carol caught me off-guard one evening when she asked, "Do you miss being a cop and doing real police work?"

"No fucking way do I miss that shit," I shouted at her. "But I'll tell you one thing. I'm going to get every one of those sonsabitches for retiring me the way they did." Deep down, Carol knew that poor Billy was feeling sorry for himself.

My next assignment was in some ways the most rewarding of all. I was responsible for the safety of 100 children, their parents, teachers, and a cast of actors who were involved in the taping of a children's television show at the MITV studio in Dartmouth. There were four shows a day for five weeks, and I was on duty for every show. I was mainly focused on keeping "The Something Else Show" celebrities from being hounded. That included Al Lewis from the Munsters, Walter Gretzky (Wayne's father), and Darrell and Darrell (brothers who were silent comedians on the Bob Newhart Show). That was my job description, but looking out for the welfare of the kids was the greatest honour and challenge of all.

I took it so seriously that I didn't drink Monday through Friday the whole time I worked there for fear of endangering the children's lives. Besides, I didn't want to be stinking of alcohol around them. This was the only time I ever remained sober through my entire work shift.

For a security guard, I played an unusually active role at the MITV studio. First, I would give milk and cookies to the kids as they came in, and then I'd seat them in the taping room. Then I would introduce the characters of the show just before the tape would start to roll. Finally, I'd turn the show over to Big Al, who played the part of a gangster. Dressed in a black suit, black shirt, and a black dip hat, he referred to me as "Officer Billy: the best cop in town."

One day, by the time the last show came around, the actors were really stressed out from having to recite their lines four times a day for five weeks. When I turned the show over to Big Al, he said: "Let's give Officer Billy a big hand. The best fuckin' cop in town!" (It's a good thing it never went on air!)

You could hear a pin drop. Just as everyone was wondering if they really heard what they thought they had heard, I stepped in and said: "Now boys and girls, the dog we have on this show, I'm going to ask you not to pet it until after the show. Then you can pet the dog." Al disappeared backstage. He was so flustered and embarrassed he wouldn't come back, so I had to ad lib for a few more minutes. Finally I went backstage and told him that no one even knew what he had said. The show went on.

What I loved about this job is it gave me such a feeling of satisfaction and accomplishment. Every day the kids would thank me, and the parents and teachers told me how much they appreciated the show. After working for so many years on the waterfront where all I got was grief, I soaked up every bit of praise and recognition that came my way.

On May 11, 1990 I was working full-time as a short-order cook at my son Glenn's store. At the end of the day Carol came by to pick me up. She was quiet all the way home. I figured there was something on her mind, and that she'd speak to me when she was ready. She remained silent through dinner, and the whole time we were watching TV. She went to bed early, at around ten o'clock.

I began to worry that maybe there was something wrong with the kids. Then the thought crossed my mind: maybe she's considering leaving me? Or is it my drinking? I went to bed at midnight.

Carol's coughing woke me up at six-thirty. She was choking. Something must have gone down the wrong way. I got up, kneeled in front of her on the bed, and grabbed her shoulders.

"What's the matter, Carol? Did you swallow something?" I asked, but she couldn't answer.

The choking got worse. As I was getting up to call an ambulance, Carol fell back on her pillow. Her expression was blank. I knew she was dead.

I sat beside her and held her hand. After a short time, it began to feel cold. I kissed her and told her I will always love her, and covered her up. As if on autopilot, I dialed Steven's phone number. Steven was twenty-eight at the time. He came right over.

In shock, I didn't move from my chair at the kitchen table all day. Steven made all the arrangements. Family, friends, and our minister came through the house and I stayed rooted to the chair—numb. I was in another world.

Carol was only fifty-four.

I decided not to drink through all this. The one phone call I made was to Kempton. I asked him to prescribe something that would get me through the next week, and he gave me some tiny purple pills.

Carol had died of a massive heart attack. She had been eating herself to death while I was drinking myself to death. On top of that, she was chain smoking. Carol would often hold both the new cigarette and the one she wasn't quite finished with. I never bothered her about smoking, and she never talked to me about my drinking. That was our pact.

Our thirty-six-year marriage had been a combination courtship, relationship, and partnership, but we were never equal. On days when Carol could only give forty per cent, I gave sixty per cent. On days when I could only give twenty-five per cent, she gave seventy-five per cent—and there were a lot of days like that.

Uniformed police from the Halifax Police Department, Port Police, and RCMP attended the funeral at St. Francis Church. Chief Peckford and Deputy London were there. It was the first time I saw Port Police serve as pall bearers at a civilian funeral.

My great granddaughter Courtney placing flowers on
Carol's grave, 2003. Photograph by Jason Hyson.

Two days later our families and close friends attended the graveside burial. Each of my children placed a single rose on their mother's casket. I turned down the rose that was offered to me and instead placed a kiss on my fingertips and placed my fingertips on her casket saying, "Wait for me, Carol. Some day I will join you and we will be together until the end of time."

In the years since Carol died, probably twenty people have told me that she is the most unforgettable person they've ever met.

Carol's magnetic personality would
light up the room.
Photograph by Billy Taylor.

When she used to visit her mother at the Samuel Prince Manor on Saturday afternoons, fifty to seventy-five residents would gather in the recreation room to talk to her. Carol would spend half an hour or so with them. Afterwards, they would say that a visit with her was far better than a visit with their doctor.

Whenever we went out to a reception or celebration of any kind, before long, people would gather around Carol just to talk to her. She drew them to her like a magnet.

Denny's wife, June, who knew Carol for thirty years said that she had never heard her make a negative remark about anyone, or put anyone down.

When she was working in a government office, Carol would show up about twenty minutes early and put a saying, short poem, or flower on each person's desk to give them a little boost as they start their day. That was the kind of person she was.

I couldn't bear life without her.

My children came by to gather up her clothing—thirty-six garbage bags full—and they dropped it off at Beacon House in Sackville. After that I locked myself in my house—just me, Shamus, and Cuddles. I didn't answer the door, except once a week my buddy Eric would drop off a case of forty-ouncers and a half-dozen six-packs of beer. (I was going to the liquor store too, but didn't want to buy enough to raise suspicions.)

Shamus had grown accustomed to Carol coming home from work at four-thirty. Every day at that time he would trot over to the living room wall, jump up, put his paws on the front windowpane, and wait for her.

I never had the heart to tell him: "Carol is no longer with us. She will never open the front door and walk in this house again." Instead, I'd tell him to go lie down, which he did. This ritual became the most difficult part of my day. Shamus ran up to greet her every day for a year, until the day he died.

13. DESCENT INTO HELL

I was drinking twice as much as usual, but I wasn't getting drunk. I've always been able to drink excessive amounts of booze without slurring my words, stumbling, or in any way looking drunk. My brain got drunk, but my body stayed sober. I'd drink, and drink, and drink, and stay awake, pacing up and down the hallway and living room, sometimes all night.

For the first couple of weeks, Eric kept me supplied with forty-ouncers of Silk Tassel rye. When he came back the second week, there was an empty case waiting for him. He had been the first and only person to call me a drunk, yet here he was, delivering the poison that disgusted him. After the second case, he said, "Go buy your own goddamn booze from now on."

Later, Eric told me my self-esteem and appearance went to hell after Carol died. My clothes, which had always been clean, were sloppy, and most of the time I looked grizzled because I rarely bothered to shave. Endurance had always been my strong suit. Wrestlers would say, "My God! Don't you ever get tired or weak?" On the waterfront, criminals would say, "Taylor, don't you ever sleep? You're here night and day watching us!"

It used to be an advantage. Now it was a curse because I could keep on going, without sleep.

I lived like this for six months—seeing no one, eating rarely, and drinking all the time. My 220-pound frame shrank to 172 pounds. I knew I needed to do something to get myself out of this hole so I decided to get out of the house and stay away from my drinking buddies.

Starting in March 1991 I decided to cut back on my drinking. I'd meet new people in new places, and not stay anywhere for very long. Over the next year I travelled through the Maritimes, Quebec, Ontario, New Hampshire, Vermont, and the New York area, by car and train.

I was betting on a geographical cure so I decided to move to Berwick in the Annapolis Valley, one of my favourite towns from the wrestling days. The former Chief of Police Archie Strong was now a retiree, and I also knew some of the firemen who lived there. I would find a beautiful apartment and live the life of a country gentleman. My daughter Lynn moved into my home in Sackville.

Right away, I landed a job with Valley Security. It was late 1992 and I was assigned to the Nova Scotia Liquor Commission store outlets in Wolfville, New Minas, and Kentville. Not the best way to get away from booze!

Soon after I started work at the New Minas store I noticed a clerk take out two paper coffee filters from his inside jacket pocket and stash them in his pants pocket. Bells were going off in my head but I just looked like a dumb security guard. On the waterfront, longshoremen would break the tops off cargo liquor bottles and pour the booze into a thermos or pop bottle, using a filter to screen out the broken glass. Then they wrote off the booze as damaged goods which was paid for by the insurance companies.

About a week later I was talking to a Liquor Commission inspector at one of the other outlets. I told him the staff might be stealing booze but I needed permission to search lunch pails and brown paper bags. I figured if he was in on it he'd go back and tell the others, so I didn't want to give him too much information.

"What do you mean?" the Inspector asked.

"I would like permission to search..."

"You can't do that," he said, cutting me off. "The union would probably go on strike. And you know the Province of Nova Scotia. If there's one thing they don't want, it's a liquor store strike." Sizing me up, he added, "We just want you to do general security. Keep an eye on the young people, check IDs, that sort of thing."

He was either in on it, or he was just a dumb bureaucrat who didn't want to ruffle any feathers. I dropped the matter. Most nights I'd hang around until the last person left, and make sure all the doors and windows were secure. On Christmas Eve, the staff took liquor off the shelves and threw a party in the lunchroom. They didn't need to use filters because it was out in the open. They would break the bottles in time for the next shift.

I figured what the hell. If you can't beat 'em, join 'em!

A female cashier at one of the stores attracted my attention, but not just because she was a looker. Somehow, she had managed to elevate herself into a position of control at that store. I was curious about her MO. Mary knew how to take advantage of her hourglass figure. She and the manager had something going on the side that no one was supposed to know about. He was an alcoholic who was on his last legs, just about ready to collect his pension, and she was a conniving, fast-talking woman who got what she wanted. She resented the fact that I was onto her. She even complained about me to get me off her case.

She would tell me to round up the carts and put them where they belonged, and I'd reply: "You put them back. I'm not working for you, the customers, or anyone else. I'm working for the manager."

"I tell Mr. Hall what to do, so I'll tell you what to do," she snapped back at me in a razor sharp voice.

I enjoyed our exchange because it spiced up an otherwise boring day.

After living in Berwick a short time, it was obvious that my plan wasn't working.

The pain of being separated from Carol was too much to bear. I was feeling more and more pain in my head, chest, and back, but the pain in my heart was the worst. Booze wouldn't dull it. I started popping pills, along with booze—Gravol®, Tylenol®, aspirin, and anything I could find for pain at the drugstore. That didn't work either so I tried more pills and less booze. I was hoping to black out so I wouldn't remember the good times with Carol, the bad memories from my childhood, and my failures. All the pills did was pep me up. I was only sleeping a couple of hours before heading to work.

Even when I was taking twenty pills a day along with a forty-ouncer of rye, I didn't show signs of being drunk. Breath mints and a bit of Old Spice aftershave masked the smell. People would say, "Billy! Do you ever smell good!"

They didn't have a clue that I was the type of alcoholic that's the toughest to spot. There's the type who takes one drink, screws up, and gets in trouble. There's the type who drinks regularly and gets in trouble, but manages to get by somehow. And then there's the functional alcoholic. In thirty-one years on the police force, I was never late for work. At one point I went ten and a half years without using a sick day. In thirty-seven years in the wrestling business and fourteen years as a PI, I was never late for work and I never booked off sick. How many non-drinkers can say that? Yet, when a personal tragedy struck, I hit bottom.

After finishing off my forty-ouncer and a six-pack of beer, I would go to a bar and have five or six doubles, and then move on to a tavern for six or eight beers. I was careful to make sure no one would catch me drinking excessively. I'd carry a good supply of two-ounce bottles so I could duck into a washroom for another shot. I used washrooms often. Sometimes I'd park my car on an out-of-the-way dirt road where I could keep drinking.

The geographical cure had failed, but I thought maybe I could get on track in Halifax by adopting a different lifestyle. On the first of September, 1993 I packed up my belongings and drove back to the city where I rented the fanciest suite in a Bedford apartment complex. This place was well-furnished. Sitting in my office, I could look out at a spectacular view of the Bedford Basin. I could see the Ceres container pier and the MacKay Bridge from my living room window.

Since I was turning over a new leaf, I reasoned, why not throw a housewarming party? My sister Joanie and her husband Bob, Denny, and his wife, and my police friends came to help me get off to a fresh start.

There was, of course, more than enough booze to go around. I stacked up the cases of rye and beer in the kitchen cupboards, and had plenty of scotch, gin, and wine on hand so I could offer everyone their favourite drink. Everyone would think Billy boy is a real generous guy, but I overbought to make sure I would have a good supply afterwards.

Back at Pinkerton's, I took on a security detail escorting several million dollars worth of art and artifacts from Halifax to Quebec City and Montreal. Once I reached Montreal, I was going to disappear and make a new life for myself. But it wasn't the Montreal I remembered from my wrestling days in the 1950s, so I returned home.

One of the last assignments I carried out with any professionalism was a stint at the Royal Bank in Musquodoboit Harbour in March 1994. I was watching a bank vault after a fire had damaged the alarm system. From then on, everything I did got screwed up somehow. I got into stupid arguments because I always felt I was coming out on the short end of the stick.

Alcohol had taken over my brain. Instead of saying "Make no mistake about it, I wear the pants in my family," I'd say, "Make no mistake about it, I wear the clothes in my family."

While on the job I told off a female picket who was on strike at CJCH Radio. I thought nothing of it because that's how I used to talk to stevedores all the time. But when I saw Roger (my boss) heading across the radio station parking lot, I could tell what was coming. When we met face to face, he said "Billy" in a sad, low voice. I could have finished the sentence for him.

Instead of feeling bad for what I'd done, the wrestler in me got his hackles up and I saw Roger the way I used to size up a shooter: you're about to become dead fucking meat.

When Roger told me I couldn't go on acting that way I told him to stick the job up his ass. I didn't need him or the job, and I added some personal insults for good measure. We had been good friends, had been to each other's homes, had lunch together, and had been through a lot over the years.

The next time I saw him, Roger said, "What you said to me, Billy...I wish you had punched me in the mouth instead."

With my cocky sonofabitch attitude I shot back, "The next time I see you, I definitely will."

By April 1994 I had established a routine. I'd run out of booze by morning and go stand in front of the liquor store at nine forty-five (fifteen minutes before it opened). I'd pace until the door was unlocked and then go inside, the first customer of the day. I'd buy a forty-ouncer of rye and a case of Keith's. Even though it was only a five-minute drive from the liquor store to my home, I'd stop off at the tavern, which opened at ten, and down six to eight drafts to tide me over. I'd pop and chew pills as if they were peanuts, to go with the booze.

Even though I had been addicted for years, I had always disguised it to myself. Meanwhile, it had grown into a monster. As far as I knew, no one ever thought I was an alcoholic. The bums and winos were—but not Billy.

I hadn't worked since I'd mouthed off to Roger, which of course gave me more time to drink. I was having nightmares. I'd wake up and I wouldn't know what day it was.

On the morning of May 3, 1994 the telephone woke me. It was Roger.

"Billy, I'd like you to take charge of the school crosswalk guards," he said.

"What would be involved?" I asked. I had never received an assignment like this before.

"Well, school is about to close so you won't be on this long. If the guard fails to report for duty, you'll make a call on your cell phone and we'll get someone there within minutes."

I realized I would have to escort the kids across the street until the crosswalk guard arrived. Me? Responsible for the lives of children, in my condition? I figured I'd probably give the wrong hand signal and a child would get injured or possibly killed. If it had been adults it would have been fine, but not kids. I have too much respect for them.

"No, Roger, I don't think I'm interested in that," I said, trying to sound like I didn't care.

(That was the last time I spoke to Roger for several years, but he never wrote me off as a hopeless drunken bastard—like a lot of my so-called friends. In fact, he has since become one of my closest friends.)

After I hung up the phone, I thought back to the crowning glory of my career when I was honoured as the "top cop" at the Canadian Police College on October 10, 1986. In eight years I had fallen from the pinnacle—to this. I couldn't even accept a job as a fucking crosswalk guard!

Helen—the woman I was seeing—was out of town at the time. We had been going out for a couple of months. Our relationship was rocky. She had brown hair and looked a lot like Carol, minus the full figure. Helen was the kind of lady you'd look at a second time if you passed her on the street. She wore tight-fitting sweaters that showed off every curve, and her laugh was magnetic.

I had fallen for Helen, so I was blind to her tricks.

While Carol was alive, my retirement savings had been in both our names. After she passed away, I put it all in my name. Shortly after we got together, Helen started telling me I could earn a much higher rate of return on my investments. One time after I had been drinking I agreed to turn my investments over to her so she could invest for me. It's a bit of a blur, but I must have sold everything and given her the cash, a bit at a time.

She then proceeded to clean out my bank accounts.

Later I found out that she had done the same to her previous husbands. When I talked to my lawyer, he said there wasn't a thing I could do since I gave her the money.

I had built up my savings by always working, starting with odd jobs after school when I was seven years old. When I was a cop I worked two jobs, seven days a week, sometimes twenty hours a day. When Carol went back to work we had three above-average incomes.

Helen went out of town and she promised she would call the next day. She didn't call which pissed me off so I dialed the number where she was staying.

Helen said she had called but I had been too drunk to remember. I could tell from the log of incoming calls that she was lying.

"You're nothing but a fucking drunk," she said. "Go to hell." And she hung up. No one *ever* talks to Billy Taylor like that! So I had another drink.

The next morning I was sitting at the coffee counter at my son Glenn's store, trying to get a handle on what was happening to me. Doris walked in. She was a married lady with three children. We had known each another for about four years. Like Helen, Doris reminded me of Carol in a lot of ways—mostly her warm smile and her good looks. Only this time she wasn't smiling.

She walked up to the counter and sat down facing me. I had never seen her look so stern. She clasped her hands over one of mine and looked me in the eyes. It goddamn nearly shocked me to death. She looked at me like *she knew* what was going on.

"Billy, I want to take you to a recovery group," she said, just like that.

Recovery group? What the hell is she talking about? "Recovery from what?" I asked.

"Recovery from alcoholism," she replied in a strangely even voice.

I came unglued. Me? Billy Taylor? The wrestling star? The cop? The PI? Go to a group of drunks and bums? I stood up, trembling. Glaring down at her, I barked, "How dare you say a thing like that to me." I grabbed her arm and hauled her out of the booth. "Now, you fuck off out of here and don't come back with shit like that again!" I walked her to the door.

Doris climbed into her car. She had turned away from me, but I could tell she was crying by the way her head would jerk back every now and again.

The next day I was sitting in my spot at the counter when Mother Teresa, Little Miss Florence Nightingale, Miss Bleeding Heart walked in. She was carrying something in a large brown paper bag. I figured she was going to give me a bottle and tell me to go drink myself to death. When she came up to me she said slowly, as if choosing every word carefully, "Billy, I promise I will not speak to you again about going to recovery group with me. I'd like to give you this book. I wrote you a letter inside the front cover. Read it before it's too late." I looked in the bag and saw a large blue book. 'What the hell do I need a book for?' I wondered. I laid it down by my jacket so I'd remember to take it home.

That night as I was pounding back the rye I was thinking about what Doris had said. She'd called me an alcoholic! Was she crazy?

14. WANDERING AROUND IN THE DARK

I was sitting in my apartment in a stupor. It wasn't a drunken stupor, or maybe it was, who the hell knows? Nothing made sense. Whatever I tried to do, I hit a wall...the geographical cure, working for Roger, you name it. I didn't know what was happening to me, and I was scared.

I was thinking about killing myself...but then realized I'd probably bungle that too.

Just then, the brown paper bag Doris had given me caught my eye. 'Now, why in the hell would she give me a book?' I wondered. Reaching over, I pulled the blue hardback out of the bag and opened it. A handwritten letter fell to the floor. I picked it up, carefully unfolded the notepaper, and began to read the small blue letters.

Doris was telling me that I can't deal with my drinking problem alone, and that if I don't start dealing with it, I'll either go crazy or end up dead. She said by attending the recovery group meetings, I'd see a lot of other people who are struggling just like me. She invited me to call her anytime I feel lonely, or meet her in the parking lot outside any of the meeting places.

Two lines caught my attention because I'd never heard anything like this before. "I know if God permits, you will become a key human being in the lives of other suffering alcoholics," and "I admire the many qualities that you possess and wish you will one day use the power you have within you to change the course of many lives, but first, your own life."

Me? Change someone else's life? Did this have something to do with God? I sat there trying to digest it all. This wasn't bullshit. She had written it from the heart. I needed to pay attention to something here.

I looked up at the twenty or so plaques and certificates on the wall of my office. At first they were a blur, but I kept staring at them, and recalled each one.

'Thank you for Thirty-one years of service on behalf of the Government of Canada, signed: the Prime Minister of Canada, Brian Mulroney.'

'Thank you for twenty years of loyal service—the Governor General of Canada.'

'Thirty-one years of loyalty and dedication to the police profession in Nova Scotia—Joe Ross, Executive Director, Police Association of Nova Scotia.'

Next to that was the gold RCMP plaque and the letter from the Canadian Police College. Even though I had planned to pass all of these on to my children and my grandchildren, I was thinking of taking them into the backyard and burning them like I had burned my wrestling gear seven years earlier. That way, I would never be reminded of my ruined police career.

Then there was silence.

Suddenly, I felt peaceful. The usual ringing in my head was gone. It seemed that someone was there with me, even though I knew I was alone. I was both nervous and relaxed. I picked up the phone and dialed Doris' number. It rang three times before she answered.

"Hullo? Is there anyone there?" she asked anxiously. After a few seconds, she said, "Is that you, Billy?"

"Yes, it's me, Doris. I'll go with you to that recovery group." I hung up before she could answer.

At my first meeting I was like a fish out of water. I was kicking myself the whole time, but I kept going—to impress Doris.

Then, one evening, she cancelled on me. Feeling sorry for myself, I got in the car and drove half an hour to Windsor to my own "meeting". I pulled into a liquor store, bought a forty-ouncer and a six-pack, and put them on the passenger seat. I wanted to forget everything that had happened over the past three weeks. The whole recovery thing with Doris had ended up a bust. About 100 feet down the road I pulled over and drained the rye, then the beer, thinking, 'Now, by God, everyone is going to feel sorry for me! Doris is going to regret not taking me to the meeting, and she's going to feel guilty as hell!' I was drinking both to get even, and to black out so I wouldn't have to deal with it anymore.

When I woke up, all I could see was a faint trace of light in the sky. Sunset or sunrise? My watch read four forty-five. I figured it must be morning. My mind was numb, with the exception of a couple of lines from a song that kept replaying like a broken record: 'Left or right at Oak Street. That's the choice I make every day. I don't know what takes more courage: the staying or the running away.'

This song had been popping into my head every now and again for the past several years. It's about a man who lives on Oak Street who is suffering a major burn-out due to a rocky home life and a job he hates. Every morning he drops off his kids at school, proceeds down Oak Street, and turns to go to work. Sitting at the stop sign he says to himself: 'Left or right at Oak Street. That's the choice I make every day. I don't know what takes more courage. The staying or the running away.'

These lyrics were driving me nuts! I didn't know all the words or even who sang it. I didn't even know what song it was, but I had been living on Oak Street all my life and it was time to make a choice. Should I go for more booze, or recovery? I wondered which would take more courage, and which I could actually pull off. I knew what the booze was doing to me; I was afraid I was going to lose my mind. Should I kill myself, to finish the job? A cop friend of mine had tried to do himself in not long ago, and it backfired on him. He drove his car as fast as he could into the Number Two Highway guardrail and all he managed to do was wreck the car!

Booze or recovery? Every time I opened a bottle, it was scary what happened to me. A genie would come out, and I couldn't drink it fast enough. I would start imagining all kinds of craziness. I was scared to go any further with the booze, so I chose recovery. I took the coward's way out.

Not long after that, my good friend, the clergyman Reverend Ralph Morris from Clairholm, Alberta, was visiting his sister in Halifax. He phoned to say hello and to let me know he was leaving the next day. I told him I'd drive him to the airport.

I used to make fun of Ralph when we were kids. When we met I was seven and he was twelve. He was cross-eyed, and his stare gave me the willies. I'd call him "Cockeyed Morris". Five years later I faced Ralph on the wrestling mat. He had been working out and looked like he was made of steel, but rather than punish me he gave me some pointers.

Wrestlers in 1948 (left to right): Myself, Bill Rhyno, Ralph Morris, Reg Haville (front). Ralph later became a minister.
The Halifax Mail and *The Halifax Herald*.

The next thing I knew, this tough guy had become a minister. When I started pro wrestling in the early 1950s, he was working with kids who had gotten into trouble with alcohol and drugs.

Now, it was more than forty years later. On the way to the airport I wanted to tell Ralph what a mess I had made of my life. Half crying, just before parking the car I finally spilled the beans about the booze and my thoughts about suicide. I told him I wanted my life to end. He just listened.

Inside, we were standing in the waiting area when Ralph turned to me and said, "Billy, would you mind if I said a prayer for you?"

"Say all the prayers you'd like. I don't know what bloody good they will do."

He started with "Oh Heavenly Father"...I was feeling so embarrassed—we must have looked like a couple of religious nuts. All I wanted to hear him say was "Amen". As Ralph disappeared through the gate I was thinking, 'Now, what the hell is his stupid prayer going to do for me? Since when did God ever answer any prayers of mine?'

That week I went back to AA, and I haven't had a drink since.

There were times during recovery when paranoia was my biggest stumbling block—but it was not just regular paranoia. I was afraid that my deepest, darkest secrets would be exposed. I hadn't told anyone about my character assassination files—not even Carol—and I was afraid this would come out in a moment of weakness. This is why I declined when my buddies in AA suggested I go into a twenty-eight-day detox program, and it's why it took me over two years to find a sponsor.

I'd held this information close over the years. These were files on politicians, cops (from constables to chiefs), judges, lawyers, prosecutors, law clerks, wrestlers, boxers, promoters, and even my own friends.

Character assassination sounds awfully sinister, but politicians conduct smear campaigns against their opponents all the time, and businesses try like hell to dig up the dirt on their competitors. Couples in the throes of divorce sling the mud at each other—sometimes, in front of their children.

It all started in 1969 during my Investigation course when I spent a morning learning about intelligence gathering at RCMP Headquarters in Ottawa. My fellow cops and I went on a guided tour of Interpol, the worldwide police network. I felt as if I was standing inside a bank vault looking at more money than anyone could count. I remember thinking, 'What I could do with all this!'

My first chance to apply intelligence gathering was when Chief Alex Taylor instructed me to compile dossiers on cargo watchmen to break the back of the organized theft rings. Those files turned out to be worth their weight in gold since I was able to use them to force waterfront workers to give us the goods on their partners in crime. I'll never forget the thrill I felt when I had the goods on poor Stanley.

It was all about power.

As a human being, I felt like a piece of shit doing this to Stanley. But as a cop, it was one of the most effective tools I had.

In my secret files I had information about the subject's alcohol, drug, and gambling habits, their credit rating and hobbies, and even the "good stuff": padded expense accounts, sexual habits, and infidelities. You never know when you'll need it.

For a guy who never felt powerful as a kid, power and control was at the top of my list as an adult. That's why I became a wrestler and a cop, and that's why I cultivated character assassination to an art. My original intention with these files was to use the information to blackmail the person into becoming an informant.

'Hell, this is even better than a shoot,' I used to think. 'After a shoot, the person heals over a period of time. But when you character assassinate someone, they never heal. If you hang character assassination over someone's head, they will live in fear forever.' I came to rely on my files the way I used my step-over toehold in a shoot.

As my drinking got more and more out of control, I learned to hone character assassination as if I were sharpening a straight razor on a whetstone to cut a fine hair. My MO was to first of all make sure I had proof. I was always polite and businesslike when I confronted someone, and I gave them anywhere from forty-eight hours to a week to think about what I said or showed them. That gave them a chance to think about what was hanging over their head while lying awake at night, and what might happen if they don't co-operate.

On the wrestling mat, I used to jam my left hand behind my opponent's neck and dig my fingers into the back of his neck, cutting off the blood flow to his head. With my right hand I'd grab his left biceps and drive my thumb into the centre to paralyze his left arm. Then I'd drive the top of my head under his chin and shove him all over the mat like I was a bulldozer. This gave him a lot of time to realize that he was losing his wind, energy, and staying power. Then, when I felt the time was right, I'd throw him on the mat to finish him off.

With character assassination, by the time I paid a second visit, the person was usually ready to cooperate. When the Chief called me "gutless" in front of my men, that was character assassination—but he couldn't back it up. So I went to the Director General and squealed on (character assassinated) him, but I had a witness who could corroborate my story.

Then the Department turned the tables and character assassinated me by charging me and finding me guilty, and then demoting me two ranks. They were trying to destroy my reputation and credibility so no one would listen to my stories about theft and kickbacks on the waterfront.

Files that back up character assassination are valuable, particularly when gathered by top investigators over the course of their career. When they retire, these files are sometimes auctioned to the young investigators who then inherit contacts and informants' names that would have taken them years to compile on their own. Back in 1989, one retired investigator I know sold his files for $5,000.

When I retired, I kept my files because I intended to continue in the same line of work, only in the security business.

While I was still working as a PI, I character assassinated two of my friends in fits of rage—actions I deeply regret today. But sometimes I used my files to help people. Late in Carol's career, a source told me that Carol's supervisor was giving her a rough time at work. He was trying to put the make on her, and then giving her a hard time about her work when she didn't show an interest. After a week's investigation I wrote an anonymous letter telling him that he had been sexually harassing Carol, and he needed to back off "or a copy of this letter will be sent to your wife and boss." About a month later, Carol came home excited.

"Billy, guess what?" she said. "I've been promoted and transferred to another job!"

Carol's bully supervisor learned that revenge is served up cold.

I'd pay a visit to certain politicians and say, "So and so was going to call the press about this incident but I stopped the bastard in his tracks before he could tell anyone." They would thank me, and I'd say, "No, I'm just doing you a favour. I support your party. I don't want anything in return. Thank you."

Usually within a month a family member or relative would be looking for a job, and I'd send them to see my politician friend. They would casually mention that they were related to me.

"I know Billy," the politician would say. "He and I are good friends."

They always got the job, just as I did when I applied to work for the Port Police.

On the downside, my character assassination secret kept me from finding a sponsor in recovery. The sponsor is someone you spill your guts to, someone who listens to all your stories—pathetic and otherwise. You're supposed to tell him your innermost secrets that cause you to drink and stay drunk. The last thing I wanted to do was tell someone that I had been keeping files on my friends.

Around this time I was going out with a thirty-year-old secretary who had just started in recovery. Out of the blue she asked, "Billy, why would someone say, 'Watch yourself if you're going out with Billy!'"

"That could have been someone I arrested at one time," I replied, "or maybe I DQ'd (disqualified) their hero in a wrestling match. A lot of people get pissed off at me."

"I hope you're not going to arrest or DQ me," she said. It gave me the shivers. I figured someone in recovery must already be onto me. Maybe they're spreading rumours that I'm going to character assassinate everyone.

Well, I told myself, if anyone fucks with me, maybe I will!

No one's going to make Billy Taylor feel guilty about what he's been doing all these years! Nope, I thought, I'll take it to my grave.

15. THERE BUT FOR THE GRACE OF GOD...

In AA, one thought kept coming back to haunt me. It was about Director General Cassidy. He had been in charge during my whole psycho testing nightmare and it bothered me a great deal that I had demanded his apology. I paid a visit to my sponsor, Ron.

"Billy, carrying a personal grudge against someone is like having a cancer that will eat at you and destroy you," he said. "But before that happens, you just might come up with a great reason to go back to the bottle. Start amends now!"

The idea of making amends and changing relationships was frightening. No matter how bad the relationship was, I didn't want it to change because I didn't know if I could handle it. My plan was to settle the score with one person, and then tell Ron I was done making amends.

I went to the local hardware store and walked into Tom's office. Tom and I had gotten into an argument the previous week. I walked away saying, "I'll never speak to you again as long as I live. You're not worth talking to."

Standing in front of him unannounced and unexpected, I said, "I'd like to have one or two words with you if I could, Tom." He looked at me blankly and sat back in his chair, hands clasped behind his neck. Tom was a tall, thin, balding guy who always dominated the conversation and put great stock in his own opinions.

"I had a few words with you a few days back and I said some things that I shouldn't have said," I began, testing the waters. "I'd like to apologize, and say that I'm sorry for what happened. And I hope we can be friends again."

"OK," he said quickly. When we shook hands I could tell that he hadn't accepted my apology, and that he had no intention of changing his mind about anything. I've shaken hands with a lot of people—as a cop, wrestler, and PI. I know when it's for real.

After the half-hearted handshake, Tom said, "Now I'm going to tell you something." And he lit into me for being a drunk and a phony. He was shouting about my sons and their problems, and saying my cop friend Walter was useless. "If I was his boss I'd have fired that drunken sonofabitch in two seconds." I felt like popping him one so I turned and walked out.

I phoned Ron from Tim Hortons and he came right over. My hand was shaking so much I could hardly hold my coffee cup to my mouth. After we talked, Ron told me I needed to explain to these people that this is not an opportunity for them to dump on me. Only after they agree to those terms should I proceed with my apology.

Ron asked to see my list. I had written down twenty-five names of people connected to events that went as far back as forty-five years. Some of them had died.

After scanning the list Ron asked, "Who's the hardest person here?"

"I didn't write that person down," I replied, staring at the floor.

He just looked at me.

"There's no point," I said, finally. "This happened twenty years ago. Besides, I don't know where he is, or if he's even alive. I'd have no idea how to find him."

"Bullshit!" Ron fired back. "You found your nephew when he went missing. You're a cop. Go find him and apologize."

For over a week, every time I looked at the phone I thought of Donald Cassidy, the Director General of Ports Canada. I had "put him in his place" twenty-three years earlier after being jerked around with all the psycho testing and having my gun taken away. I had always felt ashamed for insisting he sign that letter of apology—for making him get down on his knees and beg for forgiveness from Billy Taylor.

I finally picked up the phone and dialed his number. The first two times after two rings, I hung up. I was thinking of telling Ron I had tried to get through but the line was busy, but I knew he wouldn't buy it.

The next time I dialed I waited for someone to pick up. It was the same slow, drawly voice—quiet and polite, just as I remembered.

"Hello, is this Donald N. Cassidy that was with the Port Police at one time?" I asked.

"Yes."

"This is Billy Taylor of Halifax."

Silence for a moment, and then, "I don't believe I know you."

"Sergeant William Taylor, Port Police, Halifax, under Chief Alex Taylor."

"Ohhh yessss. Now I remember you."

Something about the way he said that gave me a bad feeling. If he hadn't been so polite, he would have said, "Oh yeah! You'd better believe I remember you, you sonofabitch!"

I was scared as hell he was going to tell me off so I brought up something non-threatening.

I told him I was having some problems, with drinking and with losing Carol. Then I talked about the Port Police being disbanded.

"Yes, I'm retired, Billy. I lost my wife some time ago. I know how hard it must be for you." Then he took control of the conversation. "And now I'm working with Parliament trying to stop them from disbanding the Port Police."

We talked for about an hour but I didn't feel comfortable enough to apologize. Shortly afterwards, I received a letter from him in which he praised me for the fine job I'm doing turning my life around from booze and drugs—not only to benefit myself but to benefit others. I was shocked. This was someone who wouldn't even look at me the last time I saw him, on Parliament Hill. I wrote back and then called him a few more times. Six months after my first phone call, I got up the courage.

"I have something on my mind, Donald," I began. "Back when the psychological testing was going on, I was pretty upset and I got you to write me a letter of apology and I'm very sorry I ever did that. I should have accepted the letter that was sent to me locally. I acted out of place, and this is something that has bothered me a great deal ever since."

Cassidy laughed and said, "Oh...That's water under the bridge now. As a matter of fact, I'm probably doing the same thing today with the politicians who are trying to disband the Port Police!"

In this good spirit, he accepted my apology. It felt as though the huge sacks I had been carrying on my back all these years had disappeared.

Shortly after our conversation, Cassidy died during heart surgery on the operating table. I'm sure glad Ron insisted I contact him right away!

Making my peace with Donald Cassidy was the beginning of making peace with Billy Taylor. Beating up on myself had become my habit. It was so ingrained, I never knew I was doing it. Here was something I had been beating myself up about for years, and all of a sudden, there was no problem! I began to relax in a way I hadn't before.

As for making amends with my kids, I believe it will happen with each of them at the right time. It's no good walking up to them out of the blue, and saying, "I'm sorry for not being around much while you were growing up." With them, it seems to happen a little bit at a time.

I made amends with my oldest son, Scott, on his deathbed. At forty-four, Scott passed away as a result of a single-car accident on September 17, 2000. It was the day before my forty-sixth wedding anniversary.

My son, Scott, who passed away in 2000.
Photograph by Billy Taylor.

I received a phone call that evening. Numb and stomach sick, I went to see Scott in the emergency room. He had sustained brain damage and wasn't conscious while I was with him. The doctor did not expect him to recover. I stood by his bedside and clasped his hand in mine.

"Scott, this is Dad," I said, and paused.

"I love you very much and I am very proud of you," I said, choked up with feeling.

That's when he squeezed my hand and wouldn't let go. I know he heard me, and in that moment, I felt totally at peace with him for the first time in a long while.

He passed away two days later.

Besides Scott's great love for his daughter and two grandchildren, he was deeply attached to his eleven-year-old dog, Minnie. While Scott was in hospital I took Minnie into my home and cared for her. Just as Shamus had done when Carol died, every day she would look for Scott to come through the door at supper time. She soon realized he was not coming home. Minnie died the day before Scott's funeral.

We had Minnie cremated, and her ashes spread over Scott's grave—next to Carol's grave at Oakridge Memory Gardens in Sackville.

Scott is now at peace with himself, with God, with his mother, and with Minnie. I will be joining them all one day.

Scott's grandson, Alexander (Alex) Scott Taylor, was born about a year later. He was named after two very important people in my life!

I hadn't seen Kempton for a few years so I was glad to run into him one afternoon. I told him I was in recovery, and that it had gotten really bad when Carol died. "I was beaten, and I didn't want anyone to know. The criminals and con artists didn't beat me. Booze did."

We walked around the corner and sat down for a coffee. I asked about Kemp's sisters, and if he was still working seven days a week, twenty-four hours a day. (I remember at one point he went for seven years without a vacation.) We were talking about old times when he brought up Marvin Burke and the psychological testing.

"All I knew, Billy, was that you were a policeman and you were a friend of mine, and I knew you wouldn't hurt anybody with a gun. So the idea of taking away your gun and ruining your career—it was terrible. I remember saying, 'This is devastating to Billy because he doesn't know where he is, and he doesn't have any answers.'"

"Why are you bringing this up now, Kemp?" I asked.

He shifted in his seat and looked me in the eye. "Because it never occurred to me that maybe Burke was right." If he had known then what he knew now, Kemp wouldn't have gone to bat for me the way he did. He wouldn't have stormed into Alex's office and read him the riot act, which is what really got things moving.

"You know, it makes perfect sense that I never suspected you were an alcoholic," he explained. "Your behaviour then was no different than when you were eight years old. It was always erratic!

"Billy," he continued, "I've often asked myself what has kept you going—through that awful period after Carol died and more recently, with Scott's death. That must have been terribly hard to take. I think it's the background you come from. You learned to fight, and that's what has kept you on top—fighting. It's like you've always been underwater, constantly trying to get on top to get some air. Now that you're sober, I'm sure you can do better than that."

We started talking about the differences between us. He came from an upper middle-class family and had a good education. I grew up poor and dropped out of school in Grade Six. After I got into wrestling, we lost touch. He went away to college; we had different friends. When he went into private practice, I looked him up because I needed a doctor.

Kemp recalled how I used to come bursting into his office.

"I remember one time you had a problem with your blood pressure," he said. "Those were awful sessions! You didn't know how to speak softly. You'd say, 'You're no fucking good. I'm going to get my lawyer to come here tomorrow to take away your license!' One time you needed a wart removed, and you said, rather loudly, 'I wouldn't let you cut the goddamn grass in front of my house!' And there'd be a little old lady in the next office, cowering. I don't know how much business you lost me. 'Where's that fucking quack?' you'd yell on the way in. The girls in the office loved you!"

He shook his head from side to side. "If you had had opportunity, things might have been a lot different for you, Billy," he said. "You spent the first part of your life trying to compensate for being short, so you beat up on everybody, and you went into the wrestling business. Then you spent the second half trying to overcome your troubles. You were combatting the guilt you felt for what you did in the first half."

When I was working at the Port, Eric was the only one who could see through me. He ended up staying with the Port Police another ten years after I was forced to retire. Eric was head of Criminal Intelligence at the Port until he left in December 1997. Not one to sit on his hands, he started Sagittarius Security Inc. and Alpha Safety Management Inc., where he oversees a staff of 150.

I admire Eric for his uncompromising approach towards investigations, the variety of cases he takes on, and his depth of knowledge that allows him to work in so many areas. Recently, he has handled cases involving break and enters, embezzlement, rape, and murder.

When I used to go to New Brunswick to see my lady friend Freda, I'd serve subpoenas for Eric on the side. We were having coffee in his office one day when he said, "You find people who can't be found. You're a goddamn pit bull! When you get your teeth into something, you don't stop until you're finished."

Once a shooter, always a goddamn shooter.

At 51, Eric didn't look much different than he did when we were on the force, except he'd put on weight.

Eric Mott and me, in Eric's Dartmouth Office, 2002.
Photograph by Andrew Safer.

He was thinking back on the rough times we've been through when he said, "Very few little things happen to you, Billy. Everything has been major. Taking your life is too common in our profession," he said matter-of-factly, "almost like it's the norm, and divorce is highly recommended. We spend over fifty per cent of our time at work, so the people at work are closer to us than our family. A high percentage of cops are alcoholics."

I said even with all the hell in my life since I retired, nothing compared to what we went through on shift.

"The only stress in police work comes from management," he said. "We're all trained to handle the stuff on the street, but they don't train you to handle management."

I took the last gulp of coffee and was getting up when Eric said, "You know what your greatest achievement is, Billy?"

"What?"

"Being sober."

Alcohol use is so common among policemen, I didn't begin to see it as a problem until after I left. The people in charge were in total denial. I can remember a police chief confidently saying at a press conference that *there was no alcoholism in any police force in Canada* (referring to mounted police, port police, and military police). "So where is the problem?" he asked.

"Fire the drunk and end the problem" is how they dealt with it.

In the mid-1970s, five members of the Halifax Police Department started to meet secretly in their own houses, to talk about personal problems they were having with alcohol, drugs, finances, or family matters. The group was called Peace and Hope—"Peace" for peace officers. They knew they would be fired if they came out in the open and admitted they had these problems because it states in the Code of Conduct that no member is to behave in such a way as to bring "discredit to the force". They started to meet with a minister at the Edgewood Church on Connaught Avenue.

One night I parked my car a few blocks from the church and pounded on the front door. I wanted to talk to someone about the psychological testing, some troubling family matters, and about the stress of having to hide booze all the time. No one answered the door. I hadn't notified them I'd be coming so they were probably afraid to open up.

Shortly after that, one of my police friends warned me to stay away from those meetings if I wanted to keep my job. I never went back.

One cop sought help for his alcohol problem by going to the Salvation Army. He was promptly fired. Today, he is working for the Salvation Army in Alberta, helping addicts.

When Vince MacDonald became Chief, things began to change. Vince had come up through the ranks. He knew what was really going on with alcoholism in the force. He encouraged the members to go to AA if they had a problem, saying he'd rather we were at AA sober, than on duty drunk. I didn't go because I was still in denial, blaming others (mainly Carol) when things went wrong, and believing I was invincible.

In 1984, Walter, another cop, came out of the closet and admitted himself into detox in Kentville. Clete did the same three weeks later. After he returned to work, the department tried to fire him twice, citing some of his behaviours on duty. Both times he won, but the third time he resigned.

Clete and Walter set up an underground organization which was later called the Police Employee Assistance Program. It helps cops who are addicted to alcohol or drugs, or who have family or financial problems. They continued to operate underground until 1993 when they could bring their work out in the open.

I wonder how much the Port Police's denial of alcoholism had to do with my own denial.

Sometimes Freda[11], my companion for five years, and I would go for a stroll on the waterfront. At 5' 3", she was about the same height as me. Freda was a farm girl who was heavyset, dressed plainly, and wore her white hair like a pixie.

Freda Marie Atkinson and me. Freda was born in Berwick, Nova Scotia
and lived in Miramichi in her later years. Peggys Cove,
Nova Scotia, 1999.
Photographer unknown.

One spring day we were walking along Pier 21, the entry for countless immigrants who came over from Europe after the Second World War. Today the building at Pier 21 looks nothing like it used to. It's a fancy new building that commemorates this historic landing point—the Ellis Island of Canada.

---

11 Freda passed away on April 9, 2002. "God's angels took another angel home."

Our main police office used to be located there. I reported there at the beginning of every shift. Inside the old dilapidated brick building had been the steamship checkers' hiring hall, and across from that, the shed entrance. The wooden plank floors sagged, the walls were in disrepair, dust from truck traffic was everywhere, and the movement of cargo was constant. I'd walk into the office, which was a fifteen-by twenty-five-foot room, and look for my daily assignment on the wooden railing the dispatch officer used as an open filing system. I didn't have my own desk so once I found my papers I'd catch a ride in a police car to my beat. Eight hours later, my replacement would be dropped off and I'd head back to the office.

When Alex took over in 1968, the office was relocated to Pier 21 Upper (upstairs) where carpets, nice furniture, and a secretary made it much more livable. That move was a major step up.

Our beautiful new office received its first threat in 1974 when the longshoremen went on strike. Between 200 and 300 pickets gathered at the entrance to Pier 21. Suddenly, all thirty of us cops were boxed in and at their mercy. They were threatening to burn the place down. The civilian offices were promptly emptied and staff were sent home.

Dressed in riot gear, nineteen members and I assembled at the entrance to Pier 21, ready to meet the pickets head on. Two riot squads of city cops were hiding across the street in the CNR train yard, and an RCMP squad was also on standby. We planned to meet the pickets at the entrance and allow them to push us back as far as the inside entrance to the shed. Then, the city squad would come in from behind and surprise them. If the pickets managed to take over the shed and police quarters, we would put on our gas masks and gas them out.

The Riot Squad during drill practice in the immigration building,
1972. I'm the short guy on the left. Photographer unknown.

None of that was necessary because the strike was settled after three days of negotiations. It was interesting that they put the only guy who had failed a psychological test on shotgun and tear gas duty. I was the only one on the riot squad carrying a gun!

For my first ten years as a cop, I worked out of Pier 21. It was like being in the middle of a bustling city. Ships came in twice a week carrying an average of 500 immigrants and fifty travelling passengers. The longshoremen would unload 100 tons of cargo from each ship and pile it in the sheds while the passengers' luggage was being loaded onto a truck and shuttled onto a train for points inland.

Myself leaving the National Harbours Board
precinct office at Pier 21, circa 1972.
Photograph by Carol Taylor.

Pier 21 was always humming with activity, with the immigrants all talking different languages. My biggest concern was traffic control as they groped their way in unfamiliar territory.

The movement of mail was a major operation. Overseas mail was prepared to be shipped out and US mail was loaded onto ships bound for New York City.

It was illegal to transport motor vehicles with gasoline in the tank, so passengers with cars had to deal with the unexpected inconvenience of getting their cars out of the sheds without a drop of gas! Even though we weren't supposed to let them, shipping agents would hire mobile gas trucks to service the cars in the sheds.

Gas-operated tow motors would tow four-wheeled carts overflowing with luggage and cargo. As the carts wound their way along the pavement, the wheels would fall into potholes, making a dull, grinding noise. If you had been inside for two or three hours during the workday, you could be overcome by the exhaust fumes because the building didn't have an air exchange system.

The Pier 21 smells at night or early in the morning are lodged in my memory. Picture yourself standing in an old hardware store and breathing in the scent of the lumber and building materials. It was like that, only way more exotic. The sharp, sweet smell of raw rubber, hemp rope (which smelled like smoked marijuana), and oil dripping from machinery are the smells I remember most.

Built in the horse and buggy days, Pier 21 wasn't designed for the five-ton trucks that came in and out, transporting cargo and luggage. It was especially tricky when a thirty-foot rig had to get in. At one point we cut the concrete curb on both sides of the entrance to make it easier for trucks to turn around.

As I was strolling up to Pier 21 with Freda, I was remembering all of this. The building had just been renovated, from top to bottom. Millions of dollars had been spent to memorialize Pier 21's role in Canadian and North American history. Neither of us had been inside since the grand opening. As I looked through the window, it all looked so clean! The building I knew was gone.

Just then, a young woman, probably nineteen, walked up. Her long black hair looked smart against her navy blazer. "May I help you?" she asked, a bit unsure of herself. I figured she must be a student who was working part-time. Had she not been so polite, she might have said, 'You tourists don't know what the hell this is all about, do you?'

"Hi, how are you today, miss?" I said for openers. "I used to work around here years ago. This place sure has changed!"

"What did you do?" she asked.

"Oh, I was with the Port Police."

Her blank stare and wrinkled brow told me she had no idea what I was talking about.

"The old place just doesn't look the same," I said to keep the conversation going.

"This is where all the immigrants came through," she replied, falling back on what she'd been taught. "Everything in the shed is the same as when the immigrants were here."

I was about to go inside when she said it would cost five dollars. Freda and I turned and walked away.

In the process of preserving it, they had made Pier 21 into something it had never been.

It sure wasn't the Pier 21 I knew. I've never gone back.

On January 20, 1999, when I was sixty-six years old, I was standing on Barrington Street looking across the street at what used to be the Family

Theatre. As a five- and six-year-old, it was one of my favourite hangouts. (My parents used to let me wander down by the docks and go to the movies. Since I didn't have any friends, I went alone.)

It was eight-thirty in the morning. I had put my briefcase down on the sidewalk, and I must have looked like a soft touch because two winos approached me. They were neatly dressed, in their late forties or early fifties. The shorter one, who was a little taller than me , did the talking. His unshaven face was weathered. He wore a red plaid shirt, light brown pants, a green summer jacket, and black shoes. His buddy, who was about 5' 10", wore a baseball cap.

"Excuse me, sir," the shorter one began.

I wanted to say, "You're excused. Now fuck off," but I let him talk. I was staring right at them to let them know that I knew their story. I was thinking, 'If you need some money for a coffee, what's wrong with the Sally Ann?', but instead I reached into my pocket and fished out a few dollars. I was going to give him a buck, but I dumped all the coins into his cupped hands. As they walked away I could hear them counting the change.

"Thank you. Thank you, sir," the older fella said.

I watched them walk away. They headed south on Barrington Street and turned left down Blowers Street.

My only thought was: "There but for the grace of God, go I."

EPILOGUE

After completing a draft of this book, tragedy struck again. Freda took sick with stomach cancer. Aside from Carol, Freda was my only other life partner. After several months of pain and agony, she died in the hospital in Miramichi on April 9, 2002.

Mid-morning on July 11th, I picked up *The Daily News* at the corner store. Scanning the front page, I read: **Major drug ring used metro port—police: NO SAFE HAVEN: Cops nab port workers.**

The Halifax Police had busted an international drug ring that had smuggled $100 million worth of drugs through the Port of Halifax since 1999. They had charged a crane operator, another longshoreman, and a clerk. They later received sentences of fourteen years, five-and-a-half years, and five-and-a-half years, respectively. Back in my time I had arrested the father of one of them, but the prosecutor wouldn't proceed with any of the charges so I had to let him go.

'What's new, pussycat?' I said to myself, chuckling. This was the first major crackdown on the Port's organized theft rings since I'd retired thirteen years earlier.

I wasn't surprised that the theft rings were still alive and well—"bigger and better" than in my time—since the crooks had never been caught. Comparing the old days to now, the main difference was the evolution from alcohol, clothing, appliances, and building materials, to narcotics.

Then, on August 31st, *The Globe and Mail* ran a front-page story: **Ports remain vulnerable to terror threats**. The ports mentioned were Vancouver, Montreal,

and Halifax. One line caught my eye: "Inaction for years by the federal government has allowed organized crime to infiltrate the ports and operate with vir-
tual impunity, (intelligence and customs) officers agree."

Hmmm...Maybe disbanding the Port Police wasn't such a good idea after
all! And what about tying our hands and not letting us do police work? Maybe
that wasn't such a good idea either!

A week later, on September 8, there was another front-page article, this time
in the *Sunday Herald*: **Manley blasts lax port patrol**. It quoted Deputy Prime
Minister John Manley saying "Someone isn't doing their job." This referred to
a recent *Ottawa Citizen* story. The reporter had found nothing but holes in the
Port of Halifax security system during a port visit. My buddy Eric Mott, who
had retired as Intelligence Officer at the Port some years earlier, had taken him
through every shed and every building to show him the lack of security that was
being provided by security agencies on the waterfront.

I've been doing some PI work for Eric to keep busy, so I dropped by his
Dartmouth office that afternoon, before my shift.

We reminisced about the old days.

"Having an RCMP background," Eric said, "I was a bit more suspicious than
most down there. As you know, I didn't want to make friends with anyone in
the police force."

"Tell me about it! 'I want a transfer off your shift, you fucking drunk!'" I
mimicked.

"Billy, when they forced you out, they figured you wouldn't be causing them
any more trouble—but they were wrong. When you retired, you passed on your
intelligence to the next generation of policemen. Not only do the officers work
there, but their family relations work there too, so we were able to keep building those ties. That's how we maintained continuity in the police system about
organized crime, and the structure that has developed way past where we ever
thought it would.

"I should say, we *had* continuity, but then, in the end, they didn't want police
work done. Because of the influence of organized crime and pressure from the
stevedoring companies, they chose to disband the police force. That broke the
chain of continuity. But now, we're seeing information that died five years ago
resurfacing, so I guess it's not completely broken after all."

Eric paused and shifted in his chair.

"I know, because I followed in your footsteps," he went on. "I wouldn't put
up with anyone stealing, shooting off their mouths, or taking 'loaned' money.
And I never thought two guys as headstrong as us could become good friends
over the years."

Eric is one of the few cops I've known who doesn't take any shit from anyone, and he has always had integrity in his actions.

The conversation shifted to the news of the recent drug bust.

"This was basically the same typical scenario we were always putting before the port agencies and intelligence network," Eric began. "It was about how easy it is for employees to control the shipping traffic through the Port of Halifax. That bust clearly showed how many people you need to do it: three. A guy to unload it, a guy to check it out, and a guy to tell them where to pick it up. It confirmed the entire intelligence network that we put together over the years, and it verified the names I had personally identified during my career."

Both Eric and I recalled these guys as suspects we had listed in our police notebooks while we were still working there. (Eric was suspended with pay in December 1997 for talking to the media, one month before the Port Police was disbanded in Halifax.)

As reported in *The Globe and Mail* article, the Senate committee on Canadian security and military preparedness had discovered that *thirty-nine per cent* of the longshoremen at the Port of Halifax had criminal records.

Why does that not surprise me?

Back in 1972 when I began working as a Criminal Ident. Officer, I kept files on all the port workers who had been convicted of criminal offences. It was about the same percentage then. I also fingerprinted and photographed everyone who had been *charged* with a criminal offence, and sent those records to Ottawa. Between both the convicts and the suspects, the criminal element was certainly alive and well on the Halifax waterfront! That's what made my job even more frustrating—knowing the type of people I was dealing with, and *still* not getting the back-up I needed to go after them—except when Alex was in charge.

That same *Globe and Mail* article also reported that Customs officials who inspect suspicious cargo were being intimidated on a regular basis.

That's not news either!

"When the cargo was stored on pallets in the sheds, they used to intimidate us with the forklifts," I recalled with Eric. "I got in shit one time because I told one guy I was going to shoot him off the forks."

Of course, intimidation and harassment didn't stop on the ground level. Management did their fair share, as I had found out through the psychological testing and then when they wanted me to "retire". And I wasn't alone.

Bruce Brine, who replaced Peckford as Chief in 1993, was fired in 1995 when, on his own initiative, he was investigating allegations of kickbacks to port officials, and their suspected association with the Hell's Angels. His superiors cited misconduct as the reason for the firing. Nine years later, Bruce reached a settlement with the Halifax Port Authority and Transport Canada through the Canadian Human Rights Commission.

Chief Bruce Brine, circa 1995.
Photograph by Billy Taylor.

Around the same time, in 1994-1995, at the Port of Vancouver, Canada Ports Police Superintendent Mike Toddington and his men were warning port officials about the Hells Angels' involvement at the Port.[12] Ports Canada Police was disbanded soon after.

The bureaucracy just doesn't want anyone to rock the boat.

"It was like that when I was a kid on the waterfront," I told Eric. "When my Uncle Charlie worked as a stevedore, I used to play down there. I remember him talking about the theft. Then, I started to work there and I tried to change some things. But nothing's changed, and nothing will *ever* fucking change on the waterfront."

In the summer of 2005, *The New York Times* reported that federal authorities were bringing a major lawsuit against the International Longshoremen's Association (ILA) in "what would be the most aggressive attempt ever to wrest the nation's Atlantic and Gulf Coast docks and the union that represents their workers from what prosecutors say is a half-century of control by two powerful New York mob clans."[13]

(At the time that the National Harbours Board was established in 1936, according to John Davis in the book *Mafia Dynasty: The Rise and Fall of the Gambino Crime Family*, Anthony ("Tough Tony") Anastasio was gaining control of the docks in Brooklyn as vice president of the International Longshoremen's Association (ILA) and head of Local 1814. "Tough Tony" was in cahoots with his brother Albert, an underboss in the Mangano crime family and head of Murder Incorporated, a secret organization that carried out hit contracts for La Cosa Nostra in New York. "Tough Tony" was believed to be the most powerful man on the New York waterfront in the forties and fifties. According to Davis, through Anthony and Albert's association, the mob controlled the New York docks.[14])

---

12 Julian Sher and William Marsden, *The Road to Hell: How the Biker Gangs Are Conquering Canada* (Seal Books/ Random House of Canada Limited, 2003), 205-207.
13 William K. Rashbaum, "U.S. Said to Plan Rackets Lawsuit Over Dockworkers' Union", *The New York Times* (June 30, 2005).
14 Davis, John H., *Mafia Dynasty: The Rise and Fall of the Gambino Crime Family* (New York: HarperTorch, 1993), 56-64

The article about the lawsuit against the ILA reminded me of what Clary had told me *forty-seven years* earlier, my first day on the job. He said that what was going on at the Port of Halifax was controlled by the ILA President in New York City.

No matter what resources the government throws at this lawsuit, they can't win because there's *no limit* to the amount of money, power, and influence organized crime has at its disposal.

When Eric and I were talking about the drug bust, he said, "The stevedores and checkers will always control the waterfront, and the shipping in and out of this country. You can bring in all the gadgets you want, like scanners, but they'll still be doing business the same way."

There will always be crooks at the Port. It's like the Public Gardens in Halifax. They can change the flowers and the ducks, but it's always going to be the Public Gardens.